THEME & IMAGE

Book 1

**ROSS SHEPPARD
ENGLISH DEPARTMENT**

Theme & Image

AN ANTHOLOGY OF POETRY / BOOK 1

Carol Gillanders

Copp Clark Pitman
A division of Copp Clark Limited
Toronto

Carol Gillanders
Formerly Teacher of English
Parkdale Collegiate Institute.
Toronto

© Copp Clark Pitman 1976

Copp Clark Pitman
517 Wellington Street West
Toronto, Ontario
M5V 1G1

Printed and bound in Canada

ISBN 0 7730 2302 x

FOREWORD

This anthology begins with a collection of Canadian poems, in order to show students and their parents that English-speaking Canada does have a significant literary tradition, as well as a flourishing group of poets today whose works provide worthwhile and interesting reading. It is hoped that English teachers will devote a unit of study to the Canadian poetry, and will encourage students to read more widely in Canadian literature.

The Canadian poetry included here does not attempt to be a representative sample of Canadian verse; rather, it has been chosen to appeal directly to the experience and response of modern young Canadians.

Recommended for high school students in the senior grades of eleven, twelve, and thirteen, this book also includes a large selection of modern American and British poetry, because of the immediate appeal of more timely material to young people. The language of recent poetry, which can seem difficult to understand for adults, is often not so hard to interpret for students, because they are often more "in tune" with modern poets, who are generally ahead of their time in thought and expression. In addition, young people on the whole are more willing to rise to the challenge of newer modes of poetic expression because they have fewer preconceptions to overcome. Grown-ups, on the other hand, often adhere persistently to stereotyped ideas about the language and subject matter of poetry.

Although senior students should be treated primarily to more recent material, they should also be introduced to some of the universal themes that run through great literature of the past. For this reason, a selection of pre-nineteenth century poetry has been included. The criteria for this material have not necessarily been the greatness of the poets nor the representative quality of particular works, but rather the power and immediacy of certain themes that have impact and meaning in today's world.

Many high school anthologies traditionally begin with early British poetry, and then go on to include poems from writers of the United States. If there are pages left over, the editor adds a few of the more familiar Canadian selections for sentimental reasons. In addition, since a school anthology customarily begins with the earliest poems first, modern and contemporary material is generally hidden away at the back of the book. As a result, after spending a great deal of time studying the older poetry, both students and teachers are often too tired or too bored to bother with more current writing or to consider any of the Canadian poetry.

To combat these tendencies, recent poems have been intermingled with older works in this anthology in an associative arrangement rather than a chronological or geographical order. Following a special section of Canadian Poetry, a division of this anthology has been devoted to Great Themes in Poetry. Included are old and new poems, mostly British and American, along with a few Canadian selections. These poems have been grouped according to common subjects that have been given contrasting and interesting treatments by a variety of poets. Finally, a third section, Form and Language in Poetry, introduces students in a more formal way to poems which illustrate some of the traditional poetic structures and devices of language that they should be familiar with in grades eleven, twelve, and thirteen. Thus, by studying selections in all three divisions of *Theme and Image—Book One*, students should become acquainted with not only the thoughts and feelings of Canadian writers, but also the responses of a wide group of English-speaking poets towards certain common experiences. In addition, in order to get more out of what they have been reading, students by the final section of this book should begin to understand some of the more important ways poets achieve vivid and accurate expression.

The notes at the back of the book provide information about the authors and clarify certain difficult words and phrases of many of the poems. For more detailed information about the Canadian poems especially, and for suggestions for presenting themes and teaching certain poetic techniques, the teacher should read the accompanying *Guide* book, which contains a step-by-step analysis of all of the poems in the order that they appear in this anthology. The *Teachers' Guide* also includes challenging questions and interesting recommendations for further student reading on related subjects.

Additional poems selected by the same criteria may be found in *Theme and Image—Book Two*, which has been arranged entirely according to themes for the benefit of senior high school students.

I would like to thank my former high school English teacher, Mr. C. T. Fyfe, who has retired from Central Collegiate Institute in Regina, Saskatchewan, for introducing me to the project of a poetry anthology. Miss Mary A. Campbell, Co-Ordinating Consultant of English, Language Study Centre, Toronto Board of Education, the former head of the English department at Parkdale Collegiate Institute in Toronto, has also influenced me in formulating the philosophy behind this book. I also want to express my appreciation for the expert assistance of Mrs. Kathleen Repka, editor, Copp Clark Publishing Company Limited. Finally, a special thanks to my husband, Ian G. Gillanders, for encouraging me and helping me in putting together both the anthology and the *Teachers' Guide*.

C.G.

ACKNOWLEDGEMENTS

The publishers and editor are grateful for permission to reproduce the copyright poems by the following authors.

PATRICK ANDERSON: "Sleighride". Reprinted from *The White Centre* by Patrick Anderson, by permission of the Ryerson Press, Toronto.

W. H. AUDEN: "The Unknown Citizen". Reprinted from *Collected Shorter Poems* by W. H. Auden, by permission of Faber and Faber Ltd.

MARGARET AVISON: "Snow" and "Thaw". Reprinted from *Winter Sun and Other Poems*, by permission of the University of Toronto Press and the author.

STEPHEN VINCENT BENET: "Jack Ellyat". From *John Brown's Body* by Stephen Vincent Benet. Holt, Rinehart and Winston, Inc. Copyright, 1927, 1928, by Stephen Vincent Benet. Copyright renewed, 1955, 1956 by Rosemary Carr Benet. Reprinted by permission of Brandt & Brandt.

EARLE BIRNEY: "Can. Lit." and "David". By permission of McClelland and Stewart Limited, Toronto.

E. E. CUMMINGS: "Spring is like a perhaps hand". Copyright 1925 by E. E. Cummings. Reprinted from his volume, *Poems 1923-1954*, by permission of Harcourt, Brace & World, Inc.; "next to of course god america i". Copyright, 1926, by Horace Liveright; renewed, 1954, by E. E. Cummings. Reprinted from his volume, *Poems 1923-1954*, by permission of Harcourt, Brace & World, Inc.

WALTER DE LA MARE: "Sunk Lyonesse". By permission of the Literary Trustees of Walter de la Mare and the Society of Authors as their representative.

T. S. ELIOT: "The Journey of the Magi" and "The Hollow Men" from *Collected Poems 1909-1962*. By permission of Faber and Faber Ltd.

LAWRENCE FERLINGHETTI: "Just as I used to say". From Lawrence Ferlinghetti, *A Coney Island of the Mind*. Copyright 1955 by Lawrence Ferlinghetti. Reprinted by permission of New Directions Publishing Corporation.

ROBERT FINCH: "The Statue" and "Train Window". By permission of McClelland and Stewart Limited, Toronto.

ROBERT FROST: "Stopping by Woods on a Snowy Evening" and "The Road Not Taken". From *Complete Poems of Robert Frost*. Copy-

Gospel by Vachel Lindsay. Copyright The Macmillan Company 1914.

AMY LOWELL: "Night Clouds". By permission of Houghton Mifflin Company.

WILLIAM LYON MACKENZIE: "Immigrants". Acknowledgements are due to J. R. Colombo for "Immigrants" from the collection of "found poems" called *The Mackenzie Poems* (Toronto: Swan Publishing Company, 1966) by William Lyon Mackenzie and John Robert Colombo.

LOUIS MACNEICE: "Morning Sun". Reprinted from *Collected Poems* by Louis MacNeice, by permission of Faber and Faber Ltd.

JAY MACPHERSON: "The Abominable Snowman". Reprinted from *The Boatman* by permission of Oxford University Press.

ELI MANDEL: "Estevan, Saskatchewan" and "Icarus", by kind permission of Eli Mandel.

PHYLLIS MCGINLEY: "Threnody". From *Times Three* by Phyllis McGinley. Copyright © 1958 by Phyllis McGinley. Originally appeared in *The New Yorker*. Reprinted by permission of The Viking Press, Inc. "Mourning's at Eight-Thirty" from *Times Three* by Phyllis McGinley. Copyright 1947 by Phyllis McGinley. Originally appeared in *The New Yorker*. Reprinted by permission of The Viking Press, Inc.

OGDEN NASH: "Kindly Unhitch That Star, Buddy". Copyright 1935 by Ogden Nash. "Love Under the Republicans (or Democrats)". Copyright 1930 by Ogden Nash. From *Verses from 1929 On* by Ogden Nash, by permission of Little, Brown and Co.

ALDEN NOWLAN: "Warren Prior". Reprinted by permission of The Ryerson Press, Toronto.

P. K. PAGE: "The Stenographers". Reprinted from *As Ten As Twenty*, by permission of McClelland and Stewart Limited.

MARJORIE PICKTHALL: "The Pool". Reprinted from *Complete Poems of Marjorie Pickthall*, by permission of McClelland and Stewart Limited, Toronto.

WILLIAM PLOMER: "Conquistadors" and "Death of a Zulu". Reprinted from *Collected Poems* by William Plomer, by permission of Jonathan Cape Ltd.

E. J. PRATT: "The Shark", "The Ice Floes", "Sea Gulls", "Newfoundland", and "The Prize Cat" reprinted from *Collected Poems of E. J. Pratt* by permission of The Estate of E. J. Pratt, and the Macmillan Company of Canada Limited.

JOHN CROWE RANSOM: "Blue Girls". Copyright 1927 by Alfred A. Knopf, Inc. and renewed 1955 by John Crowe Ransom. Reprinted from *Selected Poems*, by John Crowe Ransom, by permission of the publisher.

CONTENTS

CANADIAN POETRY

GREAT THEMES IN POETRY

Religion

Art

FORM AND LANGUAGE IN POETRY

Poetic Forms

Poetic Language

Canadian Poetry

National Identity

THE LONELY LAND

Cedar and jagged fir
uplift sharp barbs
against the gray
and cloud-piled sky;
and in the bay
blown spume and windrift
and thin, bitter spray
snap
at the whirling sky;
and the pine trees
lean one way.

A wild duck calls
to her mate,
and the ragged
and passionate tones
stagger and fall,
and recover,
and stagger and fall,
on these stones—
are lost
in the lapping of water
on smooth, flat stones.

3

This is a beauty
of dissonance,
this resonance
of stony strand,
this smoky cry
curled over a black pine
like a broken
and wind-battered branch
when the wind
bends the tips of the pines
and curdles the sky
from the north.

This is the beauty
of strength
broken by strength
and still strong.

A. J. M. SMITH

THE PROVINCES

First, the two older ones, the bunkhouse brawnymen,
biceps and chest, lumbering over their legend:
scooping a river up in the palm of the hand,
a dangling fish, alive; kicking open a mine;
bashing a forest bald; spitting a country to crop;
for exercise before their boar breakfast,
building a city; racing, to keep in shape,
against the white-sweatered wind; and always
bragging comparisons, and reminiscing
about their fathers' even more mythic prowess,

arguing always, like puffing champions rising
from wrestling on the green.

Then, the three flat-faced blond-haired husky ones.
And the little girl, so beautiful she was named—
to avert the evil of the evil eye—
after a prince, not princess. In crossed arms cradling her,
her brothers, tanned and long-limbed.
(Great fishermen, hauling out of Atlantic
their catch and their coal
and netting with appleblossom the shoals of their sky.)

And, last, as if of another birth,
the hunchback with the poet's face; and eyes
blue as the glass he looks upon; and fruit
his fragrant knuckles and joints; of iron marrow:—
affecting always a green habit, touched with white.

Nine of them; not counting
the adopted boy of the golden complex, nor
the proud collateral albino,—nine,
a sorcery of numbers, a game's stances.

But the heart seeks one, the heart, and also the mind
seeks single the thing that makes them one, if one.
    Yet where shall one find it? In their history—
the cairn of cannonball on the public square?
Their talk, their jealous double-talk? Or in
the whim and weather of a geography
curling in drifts about the forty-ninth?
Or find it in the repute of character:
romantic as mounties? Or discover it
in beliefs that say:

this is a country of Christmas trees?

Or hear it sing
from the house with towers, from whose towers ring
bells, and the carillon of laws?
Where shall one find it? What
to name it, that is sought?
The ladder the nine brothers hold by rungs?
The birds that shine on each other? The white water
that foams from the ivy entering their eaves?

Or find it, find it, find it commonplace
but effective, valid, real, the unity
in the family feature, the not unsimilar face?

A. M. KLEIN

CAN. LIT.

Since we had always sky about,
when we had eagles they flew out
leaving no shadow bigger than wren's
to trouble our most æromantic hens.
Too busy bridging loneliness to be alone
we hacked in ties what Emily etched in bone.
We French, we English, never lost our civil war,
endure it still, a bloodless civil bore;
no wounded lying about, no Whitman wanted.
It's only by our lack of ghosts we're haunted.

EARLE BIRNEY

A COUNTRY WITHOUT A MYTHOLOGY

No monuments or landmarks guide the stranger
Going among this savage people, masks
Taciturn or babbling out an alien jargon
And moody as barbaric skies are moody.

Berries must be his food. Hurriedly
He shakes the bushes, plucks pickerel from the river,
Forgetting every grace and ceremony,
Feeds like an Indian, and is on his way.

And yet, for all his haste, time is worth nothing.
The abbey clock, the dial in the garden,
Fade like saint's days and festivals.
Months, years, are here unbroken virgin forests.

There is no law—even no atmosphere
To smooth the anger of the flagrant sun.
November skies sting sting like icicles.
The land is open to all violent weathers.

Passion is not more quick. Lightnings in August
Stagger, rocks split, tongues in the forest hiss,
As fire drinks up the lovely sea-dream coolness.
This is the land the passionate man must travel.

Sometimes—perhaps at the tentative fall of twilight—
A belief will settle that waiting around the bend
Are sanctities of childhood, that melting birds
Will sing him into a limpid gracious Presence.

The hills will fall in folds, the wilderness
Will be a garment innocent and lustrous
To wear upon a birthday, under a light
That curls and smiles, a golden-haired Archangel.

And now the channel opens. But nothing alters.
Mile after mile of tangled struggling roots,
Wild-rice, stumps, weeds, that clutch at the canoe,
Wild birds hysterical in tangled trees.

And not a sign, no emblem in the sky
Or boughs to friend him as he goes; for who
Will stop where, clumsily constructed, daubed
With war-paint, teeters some lust-red manitou?

DOUGLAS LE PAN

People and Places

THE SOLITARY WOODSMAN

When the gray lake-water rushes
Past the dripping alder-bushes,
   And the bodeful autumn wind
In the fir-tree weeps and hushes,—

When the air is sharply damp
Round the solitary camp,
   And the moose-bush in the thicket
Glimmers like a scarlet lamp,—

When the birches twinkle yellow,
And the cornel bunches mellow,
   And the owl across the twilight
Trumpets to his downy fellow,—

When the nut-fed chipmunks romp
Through the maples' crimson pomp,
   And the slim viburnum flushes
In the darkness of the swamp,—

When the blueberries are dead,
When the rowan clusters red,
   And the shy bear, summer-sleekened,
In the bracken makes his bed,—

On a day there comes once more
To the latched and lonely door,
   Down the wood-road striding silent,
One who has been here before.

Green spruce branches for his head,
Here he makes his simple bed,
   Crouching with the sun, and rising
When the dawn is frosty red.

All day long he wanders wide
With the gray moss for his guide,
   And his lonely axe-stroke startles
The expectant forest-side.

Toward the quiet close of day
Back to camp he takes his way,
   And about his sober footsteps
Unafraid the squirrels play.

On his roof the red leaf falls,
At his door the bluejay calls,
   And he hears the wood-mice hurry
Up and down his rough log walls;

Hears the laughter of the loon
Thrill the dying afternoon,—
   Hears the calling of the moose
Echo to the early moon.

And he hears the partridge drumming,
The belated hornet humming,—
   All the faint, prophetic sounds
That foretell the winter's coming.

And the wind about his eaves
Through the chilly night-wet grieves,
   And the earth's dumb patience fills him,
Fellow to the falling leaves.

CHARLES G. D. ROBERTS

IMMIGRANTS

Quebec,
April 22nd to 25th,
1831.

One forenoon
I went on board the ship
Airthy Castle,
from Bristol,
immediately after her arrival.
The passengers were in number 254,
all in the hold or steerage;
all English, from about Bristol,
Bath, Frome, Warminster, Maiden Bradley, &c.
I went below,
and truly it was a curious sight.
About 200 human beings,
male and female,
young, old, and middle-aged;

talking, singing, laughing, crying, eating, drinking, shaving,
       washing;
some naked in bed, and others dressing to go ashore;
handsome young women (perhaps some)
and ugly old men,
married and single;
religious and irreligious.
Here a grave matron
chaunting selections
from the latest edition
of the last new hymn book;
there, a brawny plough-boy
"pouring forth the sweet melody
of Robin Adair."
These settlers were poor,
but in general
they were fine-looking people,
and such as I was glad
to see come to America.
They had had a fine passage
of about a month,
and they told me
that no more ship loads of settlers
would come from the same quarter
this year.
I found that it was
the intention of many of them
to come to Upper Canada.
Fortune may smile on some,
and frown on others;
but it is my opinion
that few among them will forget
being cooped up below deck

for four weeks
in a moveable bed-room,
with 250 such fellow-lodgers
as I have endeavoured to describe.

WILLIAM LYON MACKENZIE
and JOHN ROBERT COLOMBO

WARREN PRYOR

When every pencil meant a sacrifice
his parents boarded him at school in town,
slaving to free him from the stony fields,
the meagre acreage that bore them down.

They blushed with pride when, at his graduation,
they watched him picking up the slender scroll,
his passport from the years of brutal toil
and lonely patience in a barren hole.

When he went in the Bank their cups ran over.
They marvelled how he wore a milk-white shirt
work days and jeans on Sundays. He was saved
from their thistle-strewn farm and its red dirt.

And he said nothing. Hard and serious
like a young bear inside his teller's cage,
his axe-hewn hands upon the paper bills
aching with empty strength and throttled rage.

A. NOWLAN

ESTEVAN, SASKATCHEWAN

A small town bears the mark of Cain,
Or the oldest brother with the dead king's wife
In a foul relation as viewed by sons,
Lies on the land, squat, producing
Love's queer offspring only,
Which issue drives the young
To feign a summer madness, consort with skulls,
While the farmer's chorus, a Greek harbinger,
Forecasts by frost or rings about the moon
How ill and black the seeds will grow.

This goodly frame, the earth, each of its sons,
With nature as a text, and common theme
The death of fathers, anguished in betrayal
From the first family returns a sacrifice
Of blood's brother, a splintered eyeball
Groined in the fields, scarecrow to crows.
This warns Ophelia to her morning song,
Bawdy as a lyric in a pretty brain gone bad,
While on those fields the stupid harvest lies.

ELI MANDEL

FILLING STATION

With snakes of rubber and glass thorax,
like dragons rampant,
statistical, red with ambush,
they ambuscade the highway.

Only in the hinterland, and for neighbours,
the extant blacksmith drives
archaic nails into the three-legged horse.

But on Route 7
the monsters coil and spit from iron mouths
potent saliva.

(Beyond the hills, of course,
the oxen, lyric with horns, still draw
the cart and the limping wheels.)

A. M. KLEIN

NEWFOUNDLAND

Here the tides flow,
And here they ebb;
Not with that dull, unsinewed tread of waters
Held under bonds to move
Around unpeopled shores—
Moon-driven through a timeless circuit

Of invasion and retreat;
But with a lusty stroke of life
Pounding at stubborn gates,
That they might run
Within the sluices of men's hearts,
Leap under throb of pulse and nerve,
And teach the sea's strong voice
To learn the harmonies of new floods,
The peal of cataract,
And the soft wash of currents
Against resilient banks,
Or the broken rhythms from old chords
Along dark passages
That once were pathways of authentic fires.

Red is the sea-kelp on the beach,
Red as the heart's blood,
Nor is there power in tide or sun
To bleach its stain.
It lies there piled thick
Above the gulch-line.
It is rooted in the joints of rocks,
It is tangled around a spar,
It covers a broken rudder,
It is red as the heart's blood,
And salt as tears.

Here the winds blow,
And here they die,
Not with that wild, exotic rage
That vainly sweeps untrodden shores,
But with familiar breath
Holding a partnership with life,

Resonant with the hopes of spring,
Pungent with the airs of harvest.
They call with the silver fifes of the sea,
They breathe with the lungs of men,
They are one with the tides of the sea,
They are one with the tides of the heart,
They blow with the rising octaves of dawn,
They die with the largo of dusk,
Their hands are full to the overflow,
In their right is the bread of life,
In their left are the waters of death.

Scattered on boom
And rudder and weed
Are tangles of shells;
Some with backs of crusted bronze,
And faces of porcelain blue,
Some crushed by the beach stones
To chips of jade;
And some are spiral-cleft
Spreading their tracery on the sand
In the rich veining of an agate's heart;
And others remain unscarred,
To babble of the passing of the winds.

Here the crags
Meet with winds and tides—
Not with that blind interchange
Of blow for blow
That spills the thunder of insentient seas;
But with the mind that reads assault
In crouch and leap and the quick stealth,
Stiffening the muscles of the waves.

Here they flank the harbours,
Keeping watch
On thresholds, altars and the fires of home,
Or, like mastiffs,
Over-zealous,
Guard too well.

Tide and wind and crag,
Sea-weed and sea-shell
And broken rudder—
And the story is told
Of human veins and pulses,
Of eternal pathways of fire,
Of dreams that survive the night,
Of doors held ajar in storms.

E. J. PRATT

CANOE-TRIP

What of this fabulous country
Now that we have it reduced to a few hot hours
And sun-burn on our backs?
On this south side the countless archipelagoes,
The slipway where titans sent splashing the last great
      glaciers;
And then up to the foot of the blue pole star
A wilderness,
The pinelands whose limits seem distant as Thule,
The millions of lakes once cached and forgotten,

The clearings enamelled with blueberries, rank silence about
    them;
And skies that roll all day with cloud-chimeras
To baffle the eye with portents and unwritten myths,
The flames of sunset, the lions of gold and gules.
Into this reservoir we dipped and pulled out lakes and rivers,
We strung them together and made our circuit.
Now what shall be our word as we return,
What word of this curious country?

It is good,
It is a good stock to own though it seldom pays dividends.
There are holes here and there for a gold-mine or a hydro-
    plant.
But the tartan of river and rock spreads undisturbed,
The plaid of a land with little desire to buy or sell.
The dawning light skirls out its independence;
At noon the brazen trumpets slash the air;
Night falls, the gulls scream sharp defiance;
Let whoever comes to tame this land, beware!
Can you put a bit to the lunging wind?
Can you hold wild horses by the hair?
Then have no hope to harness the energy here,
It gallops along the wind away.
But here are crooked nerves made straight,
The fracture cured no doctor could correct.
The hand and mind, reknit, stand whole for work;
The fable proves no cul-de-sac.
Now from the maze we circle back;
The map suggested a wealth of cloudy escapes;
That was a dream, we have converted the dream to act.
And what we now expect is not simplicity,
No steady breeze, or any surprise,

Orchids along the portage, white water, crimson leaves.
Content, we face again the complex task.

And yet the marvels we have seen remain.
We think of the eagles, of the fawns at the river bend,
The storms, the sudden sun, the clouds sheered downwards.
O so to move! With such immaculate decision!
O proudly as waterfalls curling like cumulus!

DOUGLAS LE PAN

Legends and Stories

THE LEGEND OF QU'APPELLE VALLEY

I am the one who loved her as my life,
    Had watched her grow to sweet young womanhood;
Won the dear privilege to call her wife,
    And found the world, because of her, was good.
I am the one who heard the spirit voice,
    Of which the paleface settlers love to tell;
From whose strange story they have made their choice
    Of naming this fair valley the "Qu'Appelle."

She had said fondly in my eager ear,
    "When Indian summer smiles with dusky lip,
Come to the lakes, I will be first to hear
    The welcome music of thy paddle dip.
I will be first to lay in thine my hand,
    To whisper words of greeting on the shore;
And when thou would'st return to thine own land,
    I'll go with thee, thy wife for evermore."

Not yet a leaf had fallen, not a tone
    Of frost upon the plain ere I set forth,
Impatient to possess her as my own,
    This queen of all the women of the north.

I rested not at even or at dawn,
   But journeyed all the dark and daylight through,
Until I reached the lakes, and, hurrying on,
   I launched upon their bosom my canoe.

Of sleep or hunger then I took no heed,
   But hastened o'er their leagues of waterways;
But my hot heart outstripped my paddle's speed
   And waited not for distance or for days,
But flew before me swifter than the blade
   Of magic paddle ever cleaved the lake,
Eager to lay its love before the maid,
   And watch the lovelight in her eyes awake.

So the long days went slowly drifting past;
   It seemed that half my life must intervene
Before the morrow, when I said at last,
   "One more day's journey and I win my queen!"
I rested then, and, drifting, dreamed the more
   Of all the happiness I was to claim,
When suddenly from out the shadowed shore,
   I heard a voice speak tenderly my name.

"Who calls?" I answered; no reply; and long
   I stilled my paddle blade and listened. Then
Above the night wind's melancholy song
   I heard distinctly that strange voice again—
A woman's voice, that through the twilight came
   Like to a soul unborn—a song unsung.
I leaned and listened—yes, she spoke my name,
   And then I answered in the quaint French tongue,

"Qu'Appelle? Qu'Appelle?" No answer, and the night
   Seemed stiller for the sound, till round me fell

The far-off echoes from the far-off height—
    "Qu'Appelle?" my voice came back, "Qu'Appelle?
        Qu'Appelle?"
This—and no more; I called aloud until
    I shuddered as the gloom of night increased,
And, like a pallid spectre wan and chill,
    The moon arose in silence in the east.

I dare not linger on the moment when
    My boat I beached beside her tepee door;
I heard the wail of women and of men,
    I saw the death-fires lighted on the shore
No language tells the torture or the pain,
    The bitterness that flooded all my life,
When I was led to look on her again,
    That queen of women pledged to be my wife.

To look upon the beauty of her face,
    The still closed eyes, the lips that knew no breath;
To look, to learn, to realize my place
    Had been usurped by my one rival—Death.
A storm of wrecking sorrow beat and broke
    About my heart, and life shut out its light
Till through my anguish some one gently spoke,
    And said, "Twice did she call for thee last night."

I started up, and bending o'er my dead,
    Asked when did her sweet lips in silence close.
"She called thy name—then passed away," they said,
    "Just on the hour whereat the moon arose."
Among the lonely lakes I go no more,
    For she who made their beauty is not there;
The paleface rears his tepee on the shore
    And says the vale is fairest of the fair.

Full many years have vanished since, but still
    The voyageurs beside the campfire tell
How, when the moonrise tips the distant hill,
    They hear strange voices through the silence swell.
The paleface loves the haunted lakes they say,
    And journeys far to watch their beauty spread
Before his vision; but to me the day,
    The night, the hour, the seasons are all dead.
I listen heartsick, while the hunters tell
    Why white men named the valley The Qu'Appelle.

E. PAULINE JOHNSON

THE FORSAKEN

I

Once in the winter
Out on a lake
In the heart of the north-land,
Far from the Fort
And far from the hunters,
A Chippewa woman
With her sick baby
Crouched in the last hours
Of a great storm.
Frozen and hungry,
She fished through the ice
With a line of the twisted
Bark of the cedar,
And a rabbit-bone hook

Polished and barbed;
Fished with the bare hook
All through the wild day,
Fished and caught nothing;
While the young chieftain
Tugged at her breasts,
Or slept in the lacings
Of the warm *tikanagan*.
All the lake surface
Streamed with the hissing
Of millions of iceflakes,
Hurled by the wind;
Behind her the round
Of a lonely island
Roared like a fire
With the voice of the storm
In the deeps of the cedars.
Valiant, unshaken,
She took of her own flesh,
Baited the fish-hook,
Drew in a grey-trout,
Drew in his fellows,
Heaped them beside her,
Dead in the snow.
Valiant, unshaken,
She faced the long distance.
Wolf-haunted and lonely,
Sure of her goal
And the life of her dear one:
Tramped for two days,
On the third in the morning,
Saw the strong bulk
Of the Fort by the river,

Saw the wood-smoke
Hang soft in the spruces,
Heard the keen yelp
Of the ravenous huskies
Fighting for whitefish:
Then she had rest.

II

Years and years after,
When she was old and withered,
When her son was an old man
And his children filled with vigour,
They came in their northern tour on the verge of winter,
To an island in a lonely lake.
There one night they camped, and on the morrow
Gathered their kettles and birch-bark,
Their rabbit-skin robes and their mink-traps,
Launched their canoes and slunk away through the islands,
Left her alone forever,
Without a word of farewell,
Because she was old and useless,
Like a paddle broken and warped,
Or a pole that was splintered.
Then, without a sigh,
Valiant, unshaken,
She smoothed her dark locks under her kerchief,
Composed her shawl in state,
Then folded her hands ridged with sinews and corded with
        veins,
Folded them across her breasts spent with the nourishing of
        children,
Gazed at the sky past the tops of the cedars,
Saw two spangled nights arise out of the twilight,

Saw two days go by filled with tranquil sunshine,
Saw, without pain, or dread, or even a moment of longing:
Then on the third great night there came thronging and
 thronging
Millions of snowflakes out of a windless cloud;
They covered her close with a beautiful crystal shroud,
Covered her deep and silent.
But in the frost of the dawn,
Up from the life below,
Rose a column of breath
Through a tiny cleft in the snow,
Fragile, delicately drawn,
Wavering with its own weakness,
In the wilderness a sign of the spirit,
Persisting still in the sight of the sun
Till day was done.
Then all light was gathered up by the hand of God and hid in
 His breast,
Then there was born a silence deeper than silence,
Then she had rest.

DUNCAN CAMPBELL SCOTT

THE ICE-FLOES

Dawn from the Foretop! Dawn from the Barrel!
A scurry of feet with a roar overhead;
The master-watch wildly pointing to Northward,
Where the herd in front of *The Eagle* was spread!

Steel-planked and sheathed like a battleship's nose,
She battered her path through the drifting floes;

Past slob and growler we drove, and rammed her
Into the heart of the patch and jammed her.
There were hundreds and thousands of seals, I'd swear,
In the stretch of that field—"white harps" to spare
For a dozen such fleets as had left that spring
To share in the general harvesting.
The first of the line, we had struck the main herd;
The day was ours, and our pulses stirred
In that brisk, live hour before the sun,
At the thought of the load and the sweepstake won.

We stood on the deck as the morning outrolled
On the fields its tissue of orange and gold,
And lit up the ice to the north in the sharp,
Clear air; each mother-seal and its "harp"
Lay side by side; and as far as the range
Of the patch ran out we saw that strange
And unimaginable thing
That sealers talk of every spring—
The "bobbing-holes" within the floes
That neither wind nor frost could close;
Through every hole a seal could dive,
And search, to keep her brood alive,
A hundred miles it well might be,
For food beneath that frozen sea.
Round sunken reef and cape she would rove,
And though the wind and current drove
The ice-fields many leagues that day,
We knew she would turn and find her way
Back to the hole, without the help
Of compass or log, to suckle her whelp—
Back to that hole in the distant floes,
And smash her way up with her teeth and her nose,

But we flung those thoughts aside when the shout
Of command from the master-watch rang out.

Assigned to our places in watches of four—
Over the rails in a wild carouse,
Two from the port and starboard bows,
Two from the broadsides—off we tore,
In the breathless rush for the day's attack,
With the speed of hounds on a caribou's track.

With the rise of the sun we started to kill,
A seal for each blow from the iron bill
Of our gaffs. From the nose to the tail we ripped them,
And laid their quivering carcasses flat
On the ice; then with our knives we stripped them
For the sake of the pelt and its lining of fat.

With three fathoms of rope we laced them fast,
With their skins to the ice to be easy to drag,
With our shoulders galled we drew them, and cast
Them in thousands around the watch's flag.
Then, with our bodies begrimed with the reek
Of grease and sweat from the toil of the day,
We made for *The Eagle,* two miles away,
At the signal that flew from her mizzen peak.
And through the night, as inch by inch
She reached the pans with the "harps" piled high,
We hoisted them up as the hours filed by
To the sleepy growl of the donkey-winch.

Over the bulwarks again we were gone,
With the first faint streaks of a misty dawn;

Fast as our arms could swing we slew them,
Ripped them, "sculped" them, roped and drew them
To the pans where the seals in pyramids rose
Around the flags on the central floes,
Till we reckoned we had nine thousand dead
By the time the afternoon had fled;
And that an added thousand or more
Would beat the count of the day before.
So back again to the patch we went
To haul, before the day was spent,
Another load of four "harps" a man,
To make the last the record pan.
And not one of us saw, as we gaffed, and skinned,
And took them in tow, that the north-east wind
Had veered off-shore; that the air was colder;
That the signs of recall were there to the south,
The flag of *The Eagle* and the long, thin smoulder
That drifted away from her funnel's mouth.
Not one of us thought of the speed of the storm
That hounded our tracks in the day's last chase
(For the slaughter was swift, and the blood was warm)
Till we felt the first sting of the snow in our face.
We looked south-east, where, an hour ago,
Like a smudge on the sky-line, some one had seen
The Eagle, and thought he had heard her blow
A note like a warning from her sirene.
We gathered in knots, each man within call
Of his mate, and slipping our ropes, we sped,
Plunging our way through a thickening wall
Of snow that the gale was driving ahead.
We ran with the wind on our shoulder; we knew
That the night had left us this only clue
Of the track before us, though with each wail

That grew to the pang of a shriek from the gale,
Some of us swore that *The Eagle* screamed
Right off to the east; to the others it seemed
On the southern quarter and near, while the rest
Cried out with every report that rose
From the strain and the rend of the wind on the floes
That *The Eagle* was firing her guns to the west.
And some of them turned to the west, though to go
Was madness—we knew it and roared, but the notes
Of our warning were lost as a fierce gust of snow
Eddied, and strangled the word in our throats.
Then we felt in our hearts that the night had swallowed
All signals, the whistle, the flare, and the smoke
To the south; and like sheep in a storm we followed
Each other; like sheep huddled and broke.

Here one would fall as hunger took hold
Of his step; here one would sleep as the cold
Crept into his blood, and another would kneel
Athwart the body of some dead seal,
And with knife and nails would tear it apart,
To flesh his teeth in its frozen heart.
And another dreamed that the storm was past,
And raved of his bunk and brandy and food,
And *The Eagle* near, though in that blast
The mother was fully as blind as her brood.
Then we saw, what we feared from the first—dark places
Here and there to the left of us, wide, yawning spaces
Of water; the fissures and cracks had increased
Till the outer pans were afloat; and we knew,
As they drifted along in the night to the east,
By the cries we heard, that some of our crew
Were borne to the sea on those pans and were lost,

And we turned with the wind in our faces again,
And took the snow with its lancing pain,
Till our eye-balls cracked with the salt and the frost;
Till only iron and fire that night
Survived on the ice as we stumbled on;
As we fell and rose and plunged—till the light
In the south and the east disclosed the dawn,
And the sea heaving with floes—and then,
The Eagle in wild pursuit of her men.

And the rest is as a story told,
Or a dream that belonged to a dim, mad past,
Of a March night and a north wind's cold,
Of a voyage home with a flag half-mast;
Of twenty thousand seals that were killed
To help to lower the price of bread;
Of the muffled beat . . . of a drum . . . that filled
A nave . . . at our count of sixty dead.

E. J. Pratt

DAVID

I

David and I that summer cut trails on the Survey,
All week in the valley for wages, in air that was steeped
In the wail of mosquitoes, but over the sunalive week-ends
We climbed, to get from the ruck of the camp, the surly

Poker, the wrangling, the snoring under the fetid
Tents, and because we had joy in our lengthening coltish

Muscles, and mountains for David were made to see over,
Stairs from the valleys and steps to the sun's retreats.

II

Our first was Mount Gleam. We hiked in the long afternoon
To a curling lake and lost the lure of the faceted
Cone in the swell of its sprawling shoulders. Past
The inlet we grilled our bacon, the strips festooned

On a poplar prong, in the hurrying slant of the sunset.
Then the two of us rolled in the blanket while round us the
    cold
Pines thrust at the stars. The dawn was a floating
Of mists till we reached to the slopes above timber, and won

To snow like fire in the sunlight. The peak was upthrust
Like a fist in a frozen ocean of rock that swirled
Into valleys the moon could be rolled in. Remotely unfurling
Eastward the alien prairie glittered. Down through the dusty

Skree on the west we descended, and David showed me
How to use the give of shale for giant incredible
Strides. I remember, before the larches' edge,
That I jumped a long green surf of juniper flowing

Away from the wind, and landed in gentian and saxifrage
Spilled on the moss. Then the darkening firs
And the sudden whirring of water that knifed down a fern-
    hidden
Cliff and splashed unseen into mist in the shadows.

III

One Sunday on Rampart's arête a rainsquall caught us,

And passed, and we clung by our blueing fingers and boot-
    nails
An endless hour in the sun, not daring to move
Till the ice had steamed from the slate. And David taught me

How time on a knife-edge can pass with the guessing of
    fragments
Remembered from poets, the naming of strata beside one,
And matching of stories from schooldays . . . We crawled
    astride
The peak to feast on the marching ranges flagged

By the fading shreds of the shattered stormcloud. Lingering
There it was David who spied to the south, remote,
And unmapped, a sunlit spire on Sawback, an overhang
Crooked like a talon. David named it the Finger.

That day we chanced on the skull and the splayed white ribs
Of a mountain goat underneath a cliff, caught
On a rock. Around were the silken feathers of hawks.
And that was the first I knew that a goat could slip.

IV

And then Inglismaldie. Now I remember only
The long ascent of the lonely valley, the live
Pine spirally scarred by lightning, the slicing pipe
Of invisible pika, and great prints, by the lowest

Snow, of a grizzly. There it was too that David
Taught me to read the scroll of coral in limestone
And the beetle-seal in the shale of ghostly trilobites,
Letters delivered to man from the Cambrian waves.

V

On Sundance we tried from the col and the going was hard.
The air howled from our feet to the smudged rocks
And the papery lake below. At an outthrust we balked
Till David clung with his left to a dint in the scarp,

Lobbed the iceaxe over the rocky lip,
Slipped from his holds and hung by the quivering pick,
Twisted his long legs up into space and kicked
To the crest. Then, grinning, he reached with his freckled
      wrist

And drew me up after. We set a new time for that climb.
That day returning we found a robin gyrating
In grass, wing-broken. I caught it to tame but David
Took and killed it, and said, "Could you teach it to fly?"

VI

In August, the second attempt, we ascended The Fortress.
By the Forks of the Spray we caught five trout and fried them
Over a balsam fire. The woods were alive
With the vaulting of mule-deer and drenched with clouds all
      the morning,

Till we burst at noon to the flashing and floating round
Of the peaks. Coming down we picked in our hats the bright
And sunhot raspberries, eating them under a mighty
Spruce, while a marten moving like quicksilver scouted us.

VII

But always we talked of the Finger on Sawback, unknown
And hooked, till the first afternoon in September we slogged

Through the musky woods, past a swamp that quivered with
     frog-song,
And camped by a bottle-green lake. But under the cold

Breath of the glacier sleep would not come, the moonlight
Etching the Finger. We rose and trod past the feathery
Larch, while the stars went out, and the quiet heather
Flushed, and the skyline pulsed with the surging bloom

Of incredible dawn in the Rockies. David spotted
Bighorns across the moraine and sent them leaping
With yodels the ramparts redoubled and rolled to the peaks,
And the peaks to the sun. The ice in the morning thaw

Was a gurgling world of crystal and cold blue chasms,
And seracs that shone like frozen salt-green waves.
At the base of the Finger we tried once and failed. Then David
Edged to the west and discovered the chimney; the last

Hundred feet we fought the rock and shouldered and kneed
Our way for an hour and made it. Unroping we formed
A cairn on the rotting tip. Then I turned to look north
At the glistening wedge of giant Assiniboine, heedless

Of handhold. And one foot gave. I swayed and shouted.
David turned sharp and reached out his arm and steadied me
Turning again with a grin and his lips ready
To jest. But the strain crumbled his foothold. Without

A gasp he was gone. I froze to the sound of grating
Edge-nails and fingers, the slither of stones, the lone
Second of silence, the nightmare thud. Then only
The wind and the muted beat of unknowing cascades.

VIII

Somehow I worked down the fifty impossible feet
To the ledge, calling and getting no answer but echoes
Released in the cirque, and trying not to reflect
What an answer would mean. He lay still, with his lean

Young face upturned and strangely unmarred, but his legs
Splayed beneath him, beside the final drop,
Six hundred feet sheer to the ice. My throat stopped
When I reached him, for he was alive. He opened his grey

Straight eyes and brokenly murmured, "over . . . over."
And I, feeling beneath him a cruel fang
Of the ledge thrust in his back, but not understanding,
Mumbled stupidly, "Best not to move," and spoke

Of his pain. But he said, "I can't move . . . If only I felt
Some pain." Then my shame stung the tears to my eyes
As I crouched, and I cursed myself, but he cried
Louder, "No, Bobbie! Don't ever blame yourself.

I didn't test my foothold." He shut the lids
Of his eyes to the stare of the sky, while I moistened his lips
From our water flask and tearing my shirt into strips
I swabbed the shredded hands. But the blood slid

From his side and stained the stone and the thirsting lichens,
And yet I dared not lift him up from the gore
Of the rock. Then he whispered, "Bob, I want to go over!"
This time I knew what he meant and I grasped for a lie

And said, "I'll be back here by midnight with ropes
And men from the camp and we'll cradle you out." But I knew

That the day and the night must pass and the cold dews
Of another morning before such men unknowing

The way of mountains could win to the chimney's top.
And then, how long? And he knew . . . and the hell of hours
After that, if he lived till we came, roping him out.
But I curled beside him and whispered, "The bleeding will stop.

You can last." He said only, "Perhaps . . . For what? A
    wheelchair,
Bob?" His eyes brightening with fever upbraided me.
I could not look at him more and said, "Then I'll stay
With you." But he did not speak, for the clouding fever.

I lay dazed and stared at the long valley,
The glistening hair of a creek on the rug stretched
By the firs, while the sun leaned round and flooded the ledge,
The moss, and David still as a broken doll.

I hunched to my knees to leave, but he called and his voice
Now was sharpened with fear. "For Christ's sake push me over!
If I could move . . . or die . . ." The sweat ran from his
    forehead
But only his head moved. A hawk was buoying

Blackly its wings over the wrinkled ice.
The purr of a waterfall rose and sank with the wind.
Above us climbed the last joint of the Finger
Beckoning bleakly the wide indifferent sky.

Even then in the sun it grew cold lying there . . . And I knew
He had tested his holds. It was I who had not . . . I looked
At the blood on the ledge, and the far valley. I looked
At last in his eyes. He breathed, "I'd do it for you, Bob."

IX

I will not remember how or why I could twist
Up the wind-devilled peak, and down through the chimney's
    empty
Horror, and over the traverse alone. I remember
Only the pounding fear I would stumble on It

When I came to the grave-cold maw of the bergschrund . . .
    reeling
Over the sun-cankered snowbridge, shying the caves
In the névé . . . the fear, and the need to make sure It was
    there
On the ice, the running and falling and running, leaping

Of gaping green-throated crevasses, alone and pursued
By the Finger's lengthening shadow. At last through the
    fanged
And blinding seracs I slid to the milky wrangling
Falls at the glacier's snout, through the rocks piled huge

On the humped moraine, and into the spectral larches,
Alone. By the glooming lake I sank and chilled
My mouth but I could not rest and stumbled still
To the valley, losing my way in the ragged marsh.

I was glad of the mire that covered the stains, on my ripped
Boots, of his blood, but panic was on me, the reek
Of the bog, the purple glimmer of toadstools obscene
In the twilight. I staggered clear to a firewaste, tripped

And fell with a shriek on my shoulder. It somehow eased
My heart to know I was hurt, but I did not faint

And I could not stop while over me hung the range
Of the Sawback. In blackness I searched for the trail by the
    creek

And found it . . . My feet squelched a slug and horror
Rose again in my nostrils. I hurled myself
Down the path. In the woods behind some animal yelped.
Then I saw the glimmer of tents and babbled my story.

I said that he fell straight to the ice where they found him,
And none but the sun and incurious clouds have lingered
Around the marks of that day on the ledge of the Finger,
That day, the last of my youth, on the last of our mountains.

Earle Birney

Winter

LATE NOVEMBER

The far-off leafless forests slowly yield
To the thick-driving snow. A little while
And night shall darken down. In shouting file
The woodmen's carts go by me homeward-wheeled,
Past the thin fading stubbles, half concealed,
Now golden-gray, sowed softly through with snow,
Where the last ploughman follows still his row,
Turning black furrows through the whitening field.
Far off the village lamps begin to gleam,
Fast drives the snow, and no man comes this way;
The hills grow wintry white, and bleak winds moan
About the naked uplands. I alone
Am neither sad, nor shelterless, nor gray,
Wrapped round with thought, content to watch and dream.

ARCHIBALD LAMPMAN

SNOW

Nobody stuffs the world in at your eyes.
The optic heart must venture: a jail-break
And re-creation. Sedges and wild rice
Chase rivery pewter. The astonished cinders quake
With rhizomes. All ways through the electric air
Trundle candy-bright disks; they are desolate
Toys, if the soul's gates seal, and cannot bear,
Must shudder under, creation's unseen freight.
But soft, there is snow's legend: colour of mourning
Along the yellow Yangtze where the wheel
Spins an indifferent stasis that's death's warning.
Asters of tumbled quietness reveal
Their petals. Suffering this starry blur
The rest may ring your change, sad listener.

MARGARET AVISON

SLEIGHRIDE

In front the horse's rump bright as a lantern
goes its gauche way—the runners squeak
on the cobbled ice. With hands plunged in the hair
of my muffled rug and a clown's red nose, I leave.

I kick my feet on the boards to keep them warm,
and pull my headband over the rims of my ears
while the driver trails his whip in the banks of snow
a-glow at the sides like waves of wonderful summers.

And my eyes cry, I smile an archaic smile
and my cheeks are rouged with aliveness and mad love
while around in a settled circle the dull hills
control the valley whose applegreen ice I leave.

Goodbye Goodbye I say and the sleigh keeps on
like shuttle in slot but crazily all the same,
working its roughhouse wood, retching its iron—
I am not anywhere now but an Adam in Time.

I wrinkle my face for the cold and cuff my flesh
and watch the fringe of the rug flap over the sides
and the shadow that slides on the drift, the quick compelled
shape of the two in blue with velvet heads.

Is anyone ever so new as upon a journey,
so full of physical news or so flashy with nerves
as one who is moved, and nakedly, freely
watches his body reel in the straight and the curves?

So I submit to this lane, to this alteration,
I cough with faith and my breath is a bulging prayer,
and I drowse in the pleasure as well as the terror of Time
with a hallelujah hello from a nest of fur.

PATRICK ANDERSON

A JANUARY MORNING

The glittering roofs are still with frost; each worn
Black chimney builds into the quiet sky
Its curling pile to crumble silently.
Far out to westward on the edge of morn,
The slender misty city towers up-borne
Glimmer faint rose against the pallid blue;
And yonder on those northern hills, the hue
Of amethyst, hang fleeces dull as horn.
And here behind me come the woodmen's sleighs
With shouts and clamorous squeakings; might and main
Up the steep slope the horses stamp and strain,
Urged on by hoarse-tongued drivers—cheeks ablaze,
Iced beards and frozen eyelids—team by team,
With frost-fringed flanks, and nostrils jetting steam.

ARCHIBALD LAMPMAN

THAW

Sticky inside their winter suits
The Sunday children stare at pools
In pavement and black ice where roots
Of sky in moodier sky dissolve.

An empty coach train runs along
The thin and sooty river flats
And stick and straw and random stones
Steam faintly when its steam departs.

Lime-water and licorice light
Wander the tumbled streets. A few
Sparrows gather. A dog barks out
Under the dogless pale pale blue.

    Move your tongue along a slat
    Of a raspberry box from last year's crate.
    Smell a saucepantilt of water
    On the coal-ash in your grate.

Think how the Black Death made men dance,
And from the silt of centuries
The proof is now scraped bare that once
Troy fell and Pompey scorched and froze.

    A boy alone out in the court
    Whacks with his hockey-stick, and whacks
    In the wet, and the pigeons flutter, and rise,
    And settle back.

MARGARET AVISON

General Subjects

THE STATUE

A small boy has thrown a stone at a statue,
And a man who threatened has told a policeman so.
Down the pathway they rustle in a row,
The boy, the man, the policeman. If you watch you

Will see the alley of trees join in the chase
And the flower-beds stiffly make after the boy,
The fountains brandish their cudgels in his way
And the sky drop a blue netting in his face.

Only the statue unmoved in its moving stillness
Holds the park as before the deed was done
On a stone axis round which the trio whirls.

Stone that endured the chisel's cutting chillness
Is tolerant of the stone at its foot of stone
And the pigeon sitting awry on its carved curls.

ROBERT FINCH

THE SHARK

He seemed to know the harbour,
So leisurely he swam;
His fin,
Like a piece of sheet-iron,
Three-cornered,
And with knife-edge,
Stirred not a bubble
As it moved
With its base-line on the water.

His body was tubular
And tapered
And smoke-blue,
And as he passed the wharf
He turned,
And snapped at a flat-fish
That was dead and floating.
And I saw the flash of a white throat,
And a double row of white teeth,
And eyes of metallic gray,
Hard and narrow and slit.

Then out of the harbour,
With that three-cornered fin
Shearing without a bubble the water
Lithely,
Leisurely,
He swam—
That strange fish,
Tubular, tapered, smoke-blue,
Part vulture, part wolf,
Part neither—for his blood was cold.

E. J. PRATT

THE PRIZE CAT

Pure blood domestic, guaranteed,
Soft-mannered, musical in purr,
The ribbon had declared the breed,
Gentility was in the fur.

Such feline culture in the gads
No anger ever arched her back—
What distance since those velvet pads
Departed from the leopard's track!

And when I mused how Time had thinned
The jungle strains within the cells,
How human hands had disciplined
Those prowling optic parallels;

I saw the generations pass
Along the reflex of a spring,
A bird had rustled in the grass,
The tab had caught it on the wing:

Behind the leap so furtive-wild
Was such ignition in the gleam,
I thought an Abyssinian child
Had cried out in the whitethroat's scream.

E. J. PRATT

THE POOL

Come with me, follow me, swift as a moth,
 Ere the wood-doves waken.
Lift the long leaves and look down, look down
Where the light is shaken,
 Amber and brown,
 On the woven ivory roots of the reed,
 On a floating flower and a weft of weed
And a feather of froth.
Here in the night all wonders are,
 Lapped in the lift of the ripple's swing,
A silver shell and a shaken star,
 And a white moth's wing.
Here the young moon when the mists unclose
Swims like the bud of a golden rose.

I would live like an elf where the wild grapes cling,
I would chase the thrush
From the red rose-berries.
All the day long I would laugh and swing
With the black choke-cherries.
I would shake the bees from the milkweed blooms,
And cool, O cool,
Night after night I would leap in the pool,
And sleep with the fish in the roots of the rush.
Clear, O clear my dreams should be made
Of emerald light and amber shade,
Of silver shallows and golden glooms.
Sweet, O sweet my dreams should be
As the dark, sweet water enfolding me
Safe as a blind shell under the sea.

MARJORIE L. C. PICKTHALL

TRANS CANADA

Pulled from our ruts by the made-to-order gale
We sprang upward into a wider prairie
And dropped Regina below like a pile of bones.

Sky tumbled upon us in waterfalls,
But we were smarter than a Skeena salmon
And shot our silver body over the lip of air
To rest in a pool of space
On the top storey of our adventure.
A solar peace
And a six-way choice.

Clouds, now, are the solid substance,
A floor of wool roughed by the wind
Standing in waves that halt in their fall
A still of troughs.

The plane, our planet,
Travels on roads that are not seen or laid
But sound in instruments on pilots' ears,
While underneath,
The sure wings
Are the everlasting arms of science.

Man, the lofty worm, tunnels his latest clay,
And bores his new career.

This frontier, too, is ours,
This everywhere whose life can only be led
At the pace of a rocket
Is common to man and man,
And every country below is an I land.

The sun sets on its top shelf,
And stars seem farther from our nearer grasp.

I have sat by night beside a cold lake
And touched things smoother than moonlight on still water,
But the moon on this cloud sea is not human,
And here is no shore, no intimacy,
Only the start of space, the road to suns.

F. R. SCOTT

HIGH FLIGHT

O, I have slipped the surly bonds of earth
    And danced the skies on laughter-silvered wings.
Sunward I've climbed and joined the tumbling mirth
    Of sun-split clouds—and done a hundred things
You have not dreamed of—wheeled and soared and swung
    High in the sunlit silence. Hovering there,
I've chased the shouting wind along and flung
    My eager craft through footless halls of air.
Up, up the long delirious, burning blue
    I've topped the wind-swept heights with easy grace
Where never lark, or even eagle flew,
    And, while with silent, lifting mind I've trod
The high untrespassed sanctity of space,
    Put out my hand and touched the face of God.

JOHN GILLESPIE MAGEE

ABOMINABLE SNOWMAN

The guardian stalking his eternal snows
With backward tread and never any sound
Afflicts the mind with horror more profound
Than caves and chasms among which he goes.

Below the snowline flourish greedy tribes
Who run with dogs to hunt him as a beast,
Then pass his pieces round in solemn feast
Accompanied with triumph-song and gibes.

The unoffending flesh they take for meat,
The hairless palms and cheeks, the white sad face,
Are human, even found in such a place:
Too like our own the still-reluctant feet.

JAY MACPHERSON

ICARUS

My father was always out in the garage
building a shining wing, a wing
that curved and flew along the edge of blue air
in that streamed and sunlit room
that smelled of oil and engines
and crankcase grease, and especially
the lemon smell of polish and cedar.

Outside there were sharp rocks, and trees,
cold air where birds fell like rocks
and screams, hawks, kites, and cranes.
The air was filled with a buzzing and flying
and the invisible hum of a bee's wings was honey
in my father's framed and engined mind.
Last Saturday we saw him at the horizon
screaming like a hawk as he fell into the sun.

ELI MANDEL

ICARUS

His friends drudged in an aeroplane factory.
The theory of speed was their sweaty talk;
And one who reclaimed rust machinery
Swore men hereafter would not run or walk.
Another crowed, pointing to his watch: "Feet?
As sure as I'm staring at Time's own face
Our offspring shall be a limbless race,
Hopping in crystal ships from street to street."
Icarus went on working on his wings.
Really he despised their tame discussion;
He'd fly, but as a god towards the sun;
And rubbing the strong wax into the strings,
He leaped into the air—to hear the chorus
Of dismayed cries: "You're bluffing, Icarus!"

IRVING LAYTON

Great Themes in Poetry

Love

HOW DO I LOVE THEE

How do I love thee? Let me count the ways.
I love thee to the depth and breadth and height
My soul can reach, when feeling out of sight
For the ends of being and ideal grace.
I love thee to the level of every day's
Most quiet need, by sun and candlelight.
I love thee freely, as men strive for right;
I love thee purely, as they turn from praise;
I love thee with the passion put to use
In my old griefs, and with my childhood's faith;
I love thee with a love I seemed to lose
With my lost saints,—I love thee with the breath,
Smiles, tears, of all my life!—and, if God choose,
I shall but love thee better after death.

ELIZABETH BARRETT BROWNING

A BIRTHDAY

My heart is like a singing bird
    Whose nest is in a watered shoot;
My heart is like an apple-tree
    Whose boughs are bent with thick-set fruit;
My heart is like a rainbow shell
    That paddles in a halcyon sea;
My heart is gladder than all these,
    Because my love is come to me.

Raise me a dais of silk and down;
    Hang it with vair and purple dyes;
Carve it in doves and pomegranates,
    And peacocks with a hundred eyes;
Work it in gold and silver grapes,
    In leaves and silver fleurs-de-lys;
Because the birthday of my life
    Is come, my love is come to me.

CHRISTINA GEORGINA ROSSETTI

JOHN ANDERSON, MY JO

John Anderson, my jo, John,
    When we were first acquent,
Your locks were like the raven,
    Your bonie brow was brent;
But now your brow is beld, John,
Your locks are like the snow;
But blessings on your frosty pow,
    John Anderson, my jo.

John Anderson, my jo, John,
　We clamb the hill thegither
And mony a cantie day, John,
　We've had wi' ane anither:
Now we maun totter down, John,
　And hand in hand we'll go,
And sleep thegither at the foot,
　John Anderson, my jo.

ROBERT BURNS

"WHEN I WAS ONE-AND-TWENTY"

When I was one-and-twenty
　I heard a wise man say,
"Give crowns and pounds and guineas
　But not your heart away;
Give pearls away and rubies
　But keep your fancy free."
But I was one-and-twenty,
　No use to talk to me.

When I was one-and-twenty,
　I heard him say again,
"The heart out of the bosom
　Was never given in vain;
'Tis paid with sighs a plenty
　And sold for endless rue."
And I am two-and-twenty,
　And oh, 'tis true, 'tis true.

A. E. HOUSMAN

SONG

Go, and catch a falling star,
   Get with child a mandrake root,
Tell me, where all past years are,
   Or who cleft the Devil's foot,
Teach me to hear mermaids singing,
Or to keep off envy's stinging,
       And find
       What wind
Serves to advance an honest mind.

If thou beest born to strange sights,
   Things invisible to see,
Ride ten thousand days and nights,
   Till age snow white hairs on thee,
Thou, when thou return'st, wilt tell me
All strange wonders that befell thee,
       And swear
       No where
Lives a woman true, and fair.

If thou findst one, let me know,
   Such a pilgrimage were sweet;
Yet do not, I would not go,
   Though at next door we might meet,
Though she were true, when you met her,
And last, till you write your letter,
       Yet she
       Will be
False, ere I come, to two, or three.

JOHN DONNE

TRUE THOMAS

True Thomas lay on Huntlie bank;
    A marvel he did see;
For there he saw a lady bright,
    Come riding down by the Eildon tree.

Her skirt was of the grass-green silk,
    Her mantle of the velvet fine;
On every lock of her horse's mane,
    Hung fifty silver bells and nine.

True Thomas he pulled off his cap,
    And bowed low down on his knee;
"All hail, thou mighty Queen of Heaven!
    For thy peer on earth could never be."

"O no, O no, Thomas," she said,
    "That name does not belong to me;
I'm but the Queen of fair Elfland,
    That hither am come to visit thee.

"Harp and carp, Thomas," she said,
    "Harp and carp along with me;
And if ye dare to kiss my lips,
    Sure of your body I will be!"

"Betide me weal, betide me woe,
    That threat shall never frighten me!"
Then he has kissed her on the lips,
    All underneath the Eildon tree.

"Now ye must go with me," she said,
    "True Thomas, ye must go with me;

And ye must serve me seven years,
　　Through weal or woe as may chance to be."

She's mounted on her milk-white steed,
　　She's taken True Thomas up behind;
And aye, whene'er her bridle rang,
　　The steed flew swifter than the wind.

O they rode on, and farther on,
　　The steed flew swifter than the wind;
Until they reached a desert wide,
　　And living land was left behind.

"Light down, light down now, Thomas," she said,
　　"And lean your head upon my knee;
Light down, and rest a little space,
　　And I will show you marvels three.

"O see ye not yon narrow road,
　　So thick beset with thorns and briers?
That is the path of righteousness,
　　Though after it but few enquires.

"And see ye not yon broad, broad road,
　　That stretches o'er the lily leven?
That is the path of wickedness,
　　Though some call it the road to heaven.

"And see ye not yon bonny road,
　　That winds about the green hillside?
That is the way to fair Elfland,
　　Where you and I this night must bide.

"But, Thomas, ye shall hold your tongue,
　　Whatever ye may hear or see;

For if ye speak word in Elfin land,
    Ye'll ne'er win back to your own countree!"

O they rode on, and farther on;
    They waded through rivers above the knee,
And they saw neither sun nor moon,
    But they heard the roaring of a sea.

It was mirk, mirk night; there was no star-light;
    They waded through red blood to the knee;
For all the blood that's shed on earth,
    Runs through the springs o' that countree.

At last they came to a garden green,
    And she pulled an apple from on high—
"Take this for thy wages, True Thomas;
    It will give thee the tongue that can never lie!"

"My tongue is my own," True Thomas he said,
    "A goodly gift ye would give to me!
I neither could to buy or sell
    At fair or tryst where I may be.

"I could neither speak to prince or peer,
    Nor ask of grace from fair ladye."
"Now hold thy peace!" the lady said,
    "For as I say, so must it be."

He has gotten a coat of the even cloth,
    And a pair of shoes of the velvet green;
And till seven years were gone and past,
    True Thomas on earth was never seen.

ANONYMOUS

LA BELLE DAME SANS MERCI

"O what can ail thee, knight-at-arms,
   Alone and palely loitering?
The sedge is withered from the lake,
   And no birds sing.

"O what can ail thee, knight-at-arms,
   So haggard and so woe-begone?
The squirrel's granary is full,
   And the harvest's done.

"I see a lily on thy brow
   With anguish moist and fever dew;
And on thy cheek a fading rose
   Fast withereth too."

"I met a lady in the meads,
   Full beautiful—a faery's child,
Her hair was long, her foot was light,
   And her eyes were wild.

"I made a garland for her head,
   And bracelets too, and fragrant zone;
She looked at me as she did love,
   And made sweet moan.

"I set her on my pacing steed
   And nothing else saw all day long,
For sideways would she lean, and sing
   A faery's song.

"She found me roots of relish sweet,
    And honey wild and manna dew,
And sure in language strange she said,
    'I love thee true!'

"She took me to her elfin grot,
    And there she wept and sighed full sore;
And there I shut her wild wild eyes
    With kisses four.

"And there she lullèd me asleep,
    And there I dreamed—Ah! woe betide!
The latest dream I ever dreamed
    On the cold hill side.

"I saw pale kings and princes too,
    Pale warriors, death-pale were they all;
Who cried— 'La Belle Dame sans Merci
    Hath thee in thrall!'

"I saw their starved lips in the gloom
    With horrid warning gapèd wide,
And I awoke and found me here
    On the cold hill side.

"And this is why I sojourn here
    Alone and palely loitering,
Though the sedge is withered from the lake,
    And no birds sing."

JOHN KEATS

LOVE UNDER THE REPUBLICANS
(OR DEMOCRATS)

Come live with me and be my love
And we will all the pleasures prove
Of a marriage conducted with economy
In the Twentieth Century Anno Donomy.
We'll live in a dear little walk-up flat
With practically room to swing a cat
And a potted cactus to give it hauteur
And a bathtub equipped with dark brown water.
We'll eat, without undue discouragement
Foods low in cost but high in nouragement
And quaff with pleasure, while chatting wittily,
The peculiar wine of Little Italy.
We'll remind each other it's smart to be thrifty
And buy our clothes for something-fifty.
We'll stand in line on holidays
For seats at unpopular matinees,
And every Sunday we'll have a lark
And take a walk in Central Park.
And one of these days not too remote
I'll probably up and cut your throat.

OGDEN NASH

Death

THE DEATH OF SAMSON

Occasions drew me early to this city;
And as the gates I enter'd with sun-rise,
The morning trumpets festival proclaim'd
Through each high street. Little I had dispatch'd
When all abroad was rumour'd that this day
Samson should be brought forth, to show the people
Proof of his mighty strength in feats and games.
I sorrow'd at his captive state, but minded
Not to be absent at that spectacle.
The building was a spacious theatre,
Half round on two main pillars vaulted high,
With seats where all the lords, and each degree
Of sort, might sit in order to behold;
The other side was open, where the throng
On banks and scaffolds under sky might stand;
I among these aloof obscurely stood.

The feast and noon grew high, and sacrifice
Had fill'd their hearts with mirth, high cheer, and wine,
When to their sports they turned. Immediately
Was Samson as a public servant brought,
In their state livery clad; before him pipes
And timbrels; on each side went armed guards,
Both horse and foot before him and behind
Archers and slingers, cataphracts and spears.
At sight of him the people with a shout
Rifted the air, clamouring their god with praise,
Who had made their dreadful enemy their thrall.

He, patient but undaunted, where they led him,
Came to the place: and what was set before him,
Which without help of eye might be assayed,
To heave, pull, draw, or break, he still perform'd
All with incredible, stupendous force,
None daring to appear antagonist.

At length, for intermission sake, they led him
Between the pillars; he his guide requested
(For so from such as nearer stood we heard),
As over-tired, to let him lean a while
With both his arms on those two massy pillars
That to the arched roof gave main support.
He unsuspicious led him; which when Samson
Felt in his arms, with head a while inclined,
And eyes fast fix'd, he stood, as one who pray'd,
Or some great matter in his mind revolved.
At last, with head erect, thus cried aloud:
"Hitherto, lords, what your commands imposed
I have performed, as reason was, obeying,
Not without wonder or delight beheld;
Now, of my own accord, such other trial
I mean to show you of my strength, yet greater,
As with amaze shall strike all who behold."
This utter'd, straining all his nerves, he bow'd;
As with the force of winds and waters pent
When mountains tremble, those two massy pillars
With horrible convulsion to and fro
He tugg'd, he shook, till down they came, and drew
The whole roof after them with burst of thunder
Upon the heads of all who sat beneath,
Lords, ladies, captains, counsellors, or priests,
Their choice nobility and flower, not only

Of this, but each Philistian city round,
Met from all parts to solemnize this feast.
Samson, with these immix'd, inevitably
Pull'd down the same destruction on himself;
The vulgar only 'scaped, who stood without.

JOHN MILTON

THE SPLENDOUR FALLS

The splendour falls on castle walls
  And snowy summits old in story;
The long light shakes across the lakes,
  And the wild cataract leaps in glory.
Blow, bugle, blow, set the wild echoes flying,
Blow, bugle; answer, echoes, dying, dying, dying.

O hark, O hear! how thin and clear,
  And thinner, clearer, farther going!
O sweet and far from cliff and scar
  The horns of Elfland faintly blowing!
Blow, let us hear the purple glens replying:
Blow, bugle; answer, echoes, dying, dying, dying.

O love, they die in yon rich sky,
  They faint on hill or field or river:
Our echoes roll from soul to soul,
  And grow for ever and for ever.
Blow, bugle, blow, set the wild echoes flying,
And answer, echoes, answer, dying, dying, dying.

ALFRED LORD TENNYSON

I FELT A FUNERAL IN MY BRAIN

I felt a funeral in my brain,
    And mourners, to and fro,
Kept treading, treading, till it seemed
    That sense was breaking through.

And when they all were seated,
    A service like a drum
Kept beating, beating, till I thought
    My mind was going numb.

And then I heard them lift a box,
    And creak across my soul
With those same boots of lead, again.
    Then space began to toll

As all the heavens were a bell,
    And Being but an ear,
And I and silence some strange race,
    Wrecked, solitary, here.

EMILY DICKINSON

JACK ELLYAT

JACK Ellyat heard the guns with a knock at his heart
When he first heard them. They were going to be in it, soon.
He wondered how it would feel. They would win, of course,
But how would it feel? He'd never killed anything much.
Ducks and rabbits, but ducks and rabbits weren't men.
He'd never even seen a man killed, a man die,
Except Uncle Amos, and Uncle Amos was old.

He saw a red sop spreading across the close
Feathers of a duck's breast—it had been all right,
But now it made him feel sick for a while, somehow.
Then they were down on the ground, and they were firing,
And that was all right—just fire as you fired at drill.
Was anyone firing at them? He couldn't tell.
There was a stone bridge. Were there rebels beyond the
     bridge?
The shot he was firing now might go and kill rebels
But it didn't feel like it.

                    A man down the line
Fell and rolled flat, with a minor coughing sound
And then was quiet. Ellyat felt the cough
In the pit of his stomach a minute.
But, after that, it was just like a man falling down.

It was all so calm except for their guns and the distant
Shake in the air of cannon. No more men were hit,
And, after a while, they all got up and marched on.
If rebels had been by the bridge, the rebels were gone,

And they were going on somewhere, you couldn't say where,
Just marching along the way that they always did.

The only funny thing was, leaving the man
Who had made that cough, back there in the trampled grass
With the red stain sopping through the blue of his coat
Like the stain on a duck's breast. He hardly knew the man
But it felt funny to leave him just lying there.

STEPHEN VINCENT BENÉT

THE NAMING OF PARTS

Today we have naming of parts. Yesterday,
We had daily cleaning. And tomorrow morning,
We shall have what to do after firing. But today,
Today we have naming of parts. Japonica
Glistens like coral in all of the neighbouring gardens,
    And today we have naming of parts.

This is the lower sling swivel. And this
Is the upper sling swivel, whose use you will see,
When you are given your slings. And this is the piling swivel,
Which in your case you have not got. The branches
Hold in the gardens their silent, eloquent gestures,
    Which in our case we have not got.

This is the safety-catch, which is always released
With an easy flick of the thumb. And please do not let me
See anyone using his finger. You can do it quite easy
If you have any strength in your thumb. The blossoms
Are fragile and motionless, never letting anyone see
    Any of them using their finger.

And this you can see is the bolt. The purpose of this
Is to open the breech, as you see. We can slide it
Rapidly backwards and forwards: we call this
Easing the spring. And rapidly backwards and forwards
The early bees are assaulting and fumbling the flowers:
    They call it easing the Spring.

They call it easing the Spring: it is perfectly easy
If you have any strength in your thumb: like the bolt,
And the breech, and the cocking-piece, and the point of
    balance,

Which in our case we have not got; and the almond-blossom
Silent in all of the gardens and the bees going backwards and
    forwards,
    For today we have naming of parts.

HENRY REED

THE DEATH OF A ZULU

The weather is mild
At the house of one of the dead.
There is fruit in the hands of his child,
There are flowers on her head.

Smoke rises up from the floor,
And the hands of a ghost
(No shadow darkens the door)
Caress the door-post.

Inside sits his wife, stunned and forsaken,
Too wild to weep;
Food lies uncooked at her feet, and is taken
By venturing fowls:
Outside, the dogs were asleep,
But they waken,
And one of them howls:
And Echo replies.

At last, with a sudden fear shaken,
The little child cries.

WILLIAM PLOMER

THE DEATH OF A TOAD

A toad the power mower caught,
Chewed and clipped off a leg, with a hobbling hop has got
  To the garden verge, and sanctuaried him
  Under the cineraria leaves, in the shade
    Of the ashen heartshaped leaves, in a dim,
      Low, and a final glade.

The rare original heartsblood goes,
Spends on the earthen hide, in the folds and wizenings, flows
  In the gutters of the banked and staring eyes. He lies
  As still as if he would return to stone,
    And soundlessly attending, dies
      Toward some deep monotone,

Toward misted and ebullient seas
And cooling shores, toward lost Amphibia's emperies.
  Day dwindles, drowning, and at length is gone
  In the wide and antique eyes, which still appear
    To watch, across the castrate lawn,
      The haggard daylight steer.

RICHARD WILBUR

Time

REMEMBER NOW THY CREATOR

Remember now thy Creator in the days of thy youth, while the evil days come not, nor the years draw nigh, when thou shalt say, I have no pleasure in them;

While the sun, or the light, or the moon, or the stars, be not darkened, nor the clouds return after the rain:

In the day when the keepers of the house shall tremble, and the strong men shall bow themselves, and the grinders cease because they are few, and those that look out of the windows be darkened, and the doors shall be shut in the streets, when the sound of the grinding is low, and he shall rise up at the voice of the bird, and all the daughters of music shall be brought low;

Also when they shall be afraid of that which is high, and fears shall be in the way, and the almond tree shall flourish, and the grasshopper shall be a burden, and desire shall fail: because man goeth to his long home, and the mourners go about the streets;

Or ever the silver cord be loosed, or the golden bowl be broken, or the pitcher be broken at the fountain, or the wheel broken at the cistern.

Then shall the dust return to the earth as it was: and the spirit shall return unto God who gave it.

Vanity of vanities, saith the preacher: all is vanity.

ECCLESIASTES XII. 1-9

FERN HILL

Now as I was young and easy under the apple boughs
About the lilting house and happy as the grass was green,
   The night above the dingle starry,
    Time let me hail and climb
   Golden in the heydays of his eyes,
And honoured among wagons I was prince of the apple towns
And once below a time I lordly had the trees and leaves
    Trail with daisies and barley
   Down the rivers of the windfall light.

And as I was green and carefree, famous among the barns
About the happy yard and singing as the farm was home,
   In the sun that is young once only,
    Time let me play and be
   Golden in the mercy of his means,
And green and golden I was huntsman and herdsman, the
    calves
Sang to my horn, the foxes on the hills barked clear and cold,
    And the sabbath rang slowly
   In the pebbles of the holy streams.

All the sun long it was running, it was lovely, the hay-
Fields high as the house, the tunes from the chimneys, it was
     air
   And playing, lovely and watery
    And fire green as grass.
   And nightly under the simple stars
As I rode to sleep the owls were bearing the farm away,
All the moon long I heard, blessed among stables, the night·
    jars
   Flying with the ricks, and the horses
    Flashing into the dark.

And then to awake, and the farm, like a wanderer white
With the dew, come back, the cock on his shoulder: it was all
   Shining, it was Adam and maiden,
      The sky gathered again
   And the sun grew round that very day.
So it must have been after the birth of the simple light
In the first, spinning place, the spellbound horses walking
      warm
   Out of the whinnying green stable
     On to the fields of praise.

And honoured among foxes and pheasants by the gay house
Under the new made clouds and happy as the heart was long,
   In the sun born over and over,
     I ran my heedless ways,
    My wishes raced through the house-high hay
And nothing I cared, at my sky blue trades, that time allows
In all his tuneful turning so few and such morning songs
   Before the children green and golden
    Follow him out of grace,

Nothing I cared, in the lamb-white days, that time would take
      me
Up to the swallow thronged loft by the shadow of my hand,
   In the moon that is always rising,
    Nor that riding to sleep
I should hear him fly with the high fields
And wake to the farm forever fled from the childless land.
Oh as I was young and easy in the mercy of his means,
   Time held me green and dying
    Though I sang in my chains like the sea.

DYLAN THOMAS

LINES ON A YOUNG LADY'S
PHOTOGRAPH ALBUM

At last you yielded up the album, which,
Once open, sent me distracted. All your ages
Matt and glossy on the thick black pages!
Too much confectionery, too rich:
I choke on such nutritious images.

My swivel eye hungers from pose to pose —
In pigtails, clutching a reluctant cat;
Or furred yourself, a sweet girl-graduate;
Or lifting a heavy-headed rose
Beneath a trellis, or in a trilby hat

(Faintly disturbing, that, in several ways) —
From every side you strike at my control,
Not least through these disquieting chaps who loll
At ease about your earlier days:
Not quite your class, I'd say, dear, on the whole.

But o, photography! as no art is,
Faithful and disappointing! that records
Dull days as dull, and hold-it smiles as frauds,
And will not censor blemishes
Like washing-lines, and Hall's Distemper boards,

But shows the cat as disinclined, and shades
A chin as doubled when it is, what grace
Your candour thus confers upon her face!
How overwhelmingly persuades
That this is a real girl in a real place,

In every sense empirically true!
Or is it just *the past?* Those flowers, that gate,
These misty parks and motors, lacerate
Simply by being over; you
Contract my heart by looking out of date.

Yes, true; but in the end, surely, we cry
Not only at exclusion, but because
It leaves us free to cry. We know *what was*
Won't call on us to justify
Our grief, however hard we yowl across

The gap from eye to page. So I am left
To mourn (without a chance of consequence)
You, balanced on a bike against a fence;
To wonder if you'd spot the theft
Of this one of you bathing; to condense,

In short, a past that no one now can share,
No matter whose your future; calm and dry,
It holds you like a heaven, and you lie
Unvariably lovely there,
Smaller and clearer as the years go by.

PHILIP LARKIN

BLUE GIRLS

Twirling your blue skirts, travelling the sward
Under the towers of your seminary,
Go listen to your teachers old and contrary
Without believing a word.

Tie the white fillets then about your lustrous hair
And think no more of what will come to pass
Than bluebirds that go walking on the grass
And chattering on the air.

Practice your beauty, blue girls, before it fail;
And I will cry with my loud lips and publish
Beauty which all our power shall never establish,
It is so frail.

For I could tell you a story which is true:
I know a lady with a terrible tongue,
Blear eyes fallen from blue,
All her perfections tarnished—yet it is not long
Since she was lovelier than any of you.

JOHN CROWE RANSOM

Nature

UPON WESTMINSTER BRIDGE

Earth has not anything to show more fair:
Dull would he be of soul who could pass by
A sight so touching in its majesty:
This city now doth, like a garment, wear
The beauty of the morning; silent, bare,
Ships, towers, domes, theatres, and temples lie
Open unto the fields, and to the sky:
All bright and glittering in the smokeless air.
Never did sun more beautifully steep
In his first splendour, valley, rock, or hill;
Ne'er saw I, never felt, a calm so deep!
The river glideth at his own sweet will:
Dear God! the very houses seem asleep;
And all that mighty heart is lying still!

WILLIAM WORDSWORTH

STOPPING BY WOODS ON A
SNOWY EVENING

Whose woods these are I think I know
His house is in the village though;
He will not see me stopping here
To watch his woods fill up with snow.

My little horse must think it queer
To stop without a farmhouse near
Between the woods and frozen lake
The darkest evening of the year.

He gives his harness bells a shake
To ask if there is some mistake.
The only other sound's the sweep
Of easy wind and downy flake.

The woods are lovely, dark and deep.
But I have promises to keep,
And miles to go before I sleep,
And miles to go before I sleep.

ROBERT FROST

SONG OF MYSELF

I

I celebrate myself, and sing myself,
And what I assume you shall assume,
For every atom belonging to me as good belongs to you.

I loaf and invite my soul,
I lean and loaf at my ease observing a spear of summer grass.

My tongue, every atom of my blood, form'd from this soil, this
    air,
Born here of parents born here from parents the same, and
    their parents the same,
I, now thirty-seven years old in perfect health begin,
Hoping to cease not till death.

Creeds and schools in abeyance,
Retiring back a while sufficed at what they are, but never
    forgotten,
I harbour for good or bad, I permit to speak at every hazard,
Nature without check with original energy.

II

Houses and rooms are full of perfumes, the shelves are
    crowded with perfumes,
I breathe the fragrance myself and know it and like it,
The distillation would intoxicate me also, but I shall not let it.

The atmosphere is not a perfume, it has no taste of the
    distillation, it is odourless,
It is for my mouth forever, I am in love with it,
I will go to the bank by the wood and become undisguised and
    naked,
I am mad for it to be in contact with me.

The smoke of my own breath,
Echoes, ripples, buzz'd whispers, love-root, silk-thread, crotch
    and vine,

My respiration and inspiration, the beating of my heart, the
    passing of blood and air through my lungs,
The sniff of green leaves and dry leaves, and of the shore and
    dark-colour'd sea-rocks, and of hay in the barn,
The sound of the belch'd words of my voice loos'd to the
    eddies of the wind,
A few light kisses, a few embraces, a reaching around of arms,
The play of shine and shade on the trees as the supple boughs
    wag,
The delight alone or in the rush of the streets, or along the
    fields and hill-sides,
The feeling of health, the full-noon trill, the song of me rising
    from bed and meeting the sun.

Have you reckon'd a thousand acres much? have you reckon'd
    the earth much?
Have you practis'd so long to learn to read?
Have you felt so proud to get at the meaning of poems?

Stop this day and night with me and you shall possess the
    origin of all poems,
You shall possess the good of the earth and sun, (there are
    millions of suns left,)
You shall no longer take things at second or third hand, nor
    look through the eyes of the dead, nor feed on the
    spectres in books,
You shall not look through my eyes either, nor take things
    from me,
You shall listen to all sides and filter them from your self.

III

A child said *What is the grass?* fetching it to me with full
    hands,

How could I answer the child? I do not know what it is any
    more than he.

I guess it must be the flag of my disposition, out of hopeful
    green stuff woven.

Or I guess it is the handkerchief of the Lord,
A scented gift and remembrancer designedly dropt,
Bearing the owner's name someway in the corners, that we
    may see and remark, and say *Whose?*

Or I guess the grass is itself a child, the produced babe of the
    vegetation.

Or I guess it is a uniform hieroglyphic,
And it means, Sprouting alike in broad zones and narrow
    zones,
Growing among black folks as among white,
Kanuck, Tuckahoe, Congressman, Cuff, I give them the same,
    I receive them the same.

And now it seems to me the beautiful uncut hair of graves.

Tenderly will I use you curling grass,
It may be you transpire from the breasts of young men,
It may be if I had known them I would have loved them,
It may be you are from old people, or from offspring taken
    soon out of their mothers' laps,
And here you are the mothers' laps.

This grass is very dark to be from the white heads of old
    mothers,
Darker than the colourless beards of old men,
Dark to come from under the faint red roofs of mouths.

O I perceive after all so many uttering tongues,
And I perceive they do not come from the roofs of mouths for
nothing.
I wish I could translate the hints about the dead young men
and women,
And the hints about old men and mothers, and the offspring
taken soon out of their laps.

What do you think has become of the young and old men?
And what do you think has become of the women and
children?

They are alive and well somewhere,
The smallest sprout shows there is really no death,
And if ever there was it led forward life, and does not wait at
the end to arrest it,
And ceas'd the moment life appear'd.

All goes onward and outward, nothing collapses,
And to die is different from what any one supposed, and
luckier.

IV

I believe a leaf of grass is no less than the journey-work of the
stars,
And the pismire is equally perfect, and a grain of sand, and
the egg of the wren,
And the tree-toad is a chef-d'oeuvre for the highest,
And the running blackberry would adorn the parlours of
heaven,
And the narrowest hinge in my hand puts to scorn all
machinery,
And the cow crunching with depress'd head surpasses any
statue,

And a mouse is miracle enough to stagger sextillions of
    infidels.

I find I incorporate gneiss, coal, long-threaded moss, fruits,
    grains, esculent roots,
And am stucco'd with quadrupeds and birds all over,
And have distanced what is behind me for good reasons,
But call any thing back again when I desire it.

In vain the speeding or shyness,
In vain the plutonic rocks send their old heat against my
    approach,
In vain the mastodon retreats beneath its own powder'd bones,
In vain objects stand leagues off and assume manifold shapes,
In vain the ocean settling in hollows and the great monsters
    lying low,
In vain the buzzard houses herself with the sky,
In vain the snake slides through the creepers and logs,
In vain the elk takes to the inner passes of the woods,
In vain the razor-bill'd auk sails far north to Labrador,
I follow quickly, I ascend to the nest in the fissure of the cliff.

V

The past and present wilt—I have fill'd them, emptied them,
And proceed to fill my next fold of the future.

Listener up there! what have you to confide to me?
Look in my face while I snuff the sidle of evening,
(Talk honestly, no one else hears you, and I stay only a minute
    longer.)

Do I contradict myself?
Very well then I contradict myself,
(I am large, I contain multitudes.)

I concentrate toward them that are nigh, I wait on the door-
slab.

Who has done his day's work? who will soonest be through
with his supper?
Who wishes to walk with me?

Will you speak before I am gone? will you prove already too
late?

VI

The spotted hawk swoops by and accuses me, he complains of
my gab and my loitering.

I too am not a bit tamed, I too am untranslatable,
I sound my barbaric yawp over the roofs of the world.

The last scud of day holds back for me,
It flings my likeness after the rest and true as any on the
shadow'd wilds,
It coaxes me to the vapour and the dusk.

I depart as air, I shake my white locks at the runaway sun,
I effuse my flesh in eddies, and drift it in lacy jags.

I bequeath myself to the dirt to grow from the grass I love,
If you want me again look for me under your boot-soles.

You will hardly know who I am or what I mean,
But I shall be good health to you nevertheless,
And filter and fibre your blood.

Failing to fetch me at first keep encouraged,
Missing me one place search another,
I stop somewhere waiting for you.

WALT WHITMAN

THE GRASS

The grass so little has to do,—
A sphere of simple green,
With only butterflies to brood,
And bees to entertain,

And stir all day to pretty tunes
The breezes fetch along,
And hold the sunshine in its lap
and bow to everything;

And thread the dews all night, like pearls,
And make itself so fine,—
A duchess were too common
For such a noticing.

And even when it dies, to pass
In odours so divine,
Like lowly spices lain to sleep,
Or spikenards perishing.

And then in sovereign barns to dwell,
And dream the days away,—
The grass so little has to do,
I wish I were a hay.

EMILY DICKINSON

THE CLOUD

I bring fresh showers for the thirsting flowers,
    From the seas and the streams;
I bear light shade for the leaves when laid
    In their noonday dreams.
From my wings are shaken the dews that waken
    The sweet buds every one,
When rocked to rest on their mother's breast,
    As she dances about the sun.
I wield the flail of the lashing hail,
    And whiten the green plains under,
And then again I dissolve it in rain,
    And laugh as I pass in thunder.

I sift the snow on the mountains below,
    And their great pines groan aghast;
And all the night 'tis my pillow white,
    While I sleep in the arms of the blast.
Sublime on the towers of my skiey bowers,
    Lightning my pilot sits;
In a cavern under is fettered the thunder,
    It struggles and howls at fits;
Over earth and ocean, with gentle motion,
    This pilot is guiding me,
Lured by the love of the genii that move
    In the depths of the purple sea;
Over the rills, and the crags, and the hills,
    Over the lakes and the plains,
Wherever he dream, under mountain or stream,
    The spirit he loves remains;
And I all the while bask in heaven's blue smile,
    Whilst he is dissolving in rains.

The sanguine sunrise, with his meteor eyes,
 And his burning plumes outspread,
Leaps on the back of my sailing rack,
 When the morning star shines dead;
As on the jag of a mountain crag.
 Which an earthquake rocks and swings,
An eagle alit one moment may sit
 In the light of its golden wings.
And when sunset may breathe, from the lit sea beneath,
 Its ardours of rest and of love,
And the crimson pall of eve may fall
 From the depth of heaven above,
With wings folded I rest, on mine airy nest,
 As still as a brooding dove.

That orbèd maiden with white fire laden,
 Whom mortals call the moon,
Glides glimmering o'er my fleece-like floor,
 By the midnight breezes strewn;
And wherever the beat of her unseen feet,
 Which only the angels hear,
May have broken the woof of my tent's thin roof,
 The stars peep behind her and peer;
And I laugh to see them whirl and flee,
 Like a swarm of golden bees,
When I widen the rent in my wind-built tent,
 Till the calm rivers, lakes, and seas,
Like strips of the sky fallen through me on high,
 Are each paved with the moon and these.

I bind the sun's throne with a burning zone,
 And the moon's with a girdle of pearl;

The volcanoes are dim, and the stars reel and swim,
  When the whirlwinds my banner unfurl.
From cape to cape, with a bridge-like shape,
  Over a torrent sea,
Sunbeam-proof, I hang like a roof, —
  The mountains its columns be.
The triumphal arch through which I march
  With hurricane, fire, and snow,
When the powers of the air are chained to my chair,
  Is the million-coloured bow;
The sphere-fire above its soft colours wove,
  While the moist earth was laughing below.

I am the daughter of earth and water,
  And the nursling of the sky;
I pass through the pores of the ocean and shores;
  I change, but I cannot die.
For after the rain when with never a stain
  The pavilion of heaven is bare,
And the winds and sunbeams with their convex gleams
  Build up the blue dome of air,
I silently laugh at my own cenotaph,
  As out of the caverns of rain,
Like a child from the womb, like a ghost from the tomb,
  I arise and unbuild it again.

PERCY BYSSHE SHELLEY

FOG

The fog comes
on little cat feet.

It sits looking
over harbour and city
on silent haunches
and then moves on.

CARL SANDBURG

SEA-GULLS

For one carved instant as they flew,
The language had no simile—
Silver, crystal, ivory
Were tarnished. Etched upon the horizon blue,
The frieze must go unchallenged, for the lift
And carriage of the wings would stain the drift
Of stars against a tropic indigo
Or dull the parable of snow.

Now settling one by one
Within green hollows or where curled
Crests caught the spectrum from the sun,
A thousand wings are furled.
No clay-born lilies of the world
Could blow as free
As those wild orchids of the sea.

E. J. PRATT

THE CAGED SKYLARK

As a dare-gale skylark scanted in a dull cage
Man's mounting spirit in his bone-house, mean house, dwells—
That bird beyond the remembering his free fells;
This in drudgery, day-labouring-out life's age.
Though aloft on turf or perch or poor low stage,
Both sing sometímes the sweetest, sweetest spells,
Yet both droop deadly sómetimes in their cells
Or wring their barriers in bursts of fear or rage.
Not that the sweet-fowl, song-fowl, needs no rest—
Why, hear him, hear him babble and drop down to his nest,
But his own nest, wild nest, no prison.
Man's spirit will be flesh-bound when found at best,
But uncumbered: meadow-down is not distressed
For a rainbow footing it nor he for his bónes rísen.

GERARD MANLEY HOPKINS

SPRING IS LIKE A PERHAPS HAND

Spring is like a perhaps hand
(which comes carefully
out of Nowhere) arranging
a window,into which people look(while
people stare
arranging and changing placing
carefully there a strange
thing and a known thing here)and

changing everything carefully

spring is like a perhaps
Hand in a window
(carefully to
and fro moving New and
Old things,while
people stare carefully
moving a perhaps
fraction of flower here placing
an inch of air there) and

without breaking anything.

E. E. CUMMINGS

SNAKE

A snake came to my water-trough
On a hot, hot day, and I in pyjamas for the heat,
To drink there.

In the deep, strange-scented shade of the great dark carob tree
I came down the steps with my pitcher
And must wait, must stand and wait; for there he was at the
trough before me.

He reached down from a fissure in the earth-wall in the gloom
And trailed his yellow-brown slackness soft-bellied down, over
the edge of the stone trough
And rested his throat upon the stone bottom,
And where the water had dripped from the tap, in a small
clearness,
He sipped with his straight mouth,

Softly drank through his straight gums, into his slack long
    body,
Silently.

Someone was before me at my water-trough,
And I, like a second-comer, waiting.

He lifted his head from his drinking, as cattle do,
And looked at me vaguely, as drinking cattle do,
And flickered his two-forked tongue from his lips, and mused
    a moment,
And stooped and drank a little more,
Being earth-brown, earth-golden from the burning bowels of
    the earth
On the day of Sicilian July, with Etna smoking.

The voice of my education said to me
He must be killed,
For in Sicily the black, black snakes are innocent, the gold are
    venomous,

And voices in me said, if you were a man
You would take a stick and break him now, and finish him off.

But must I confess how I liked him,
How glad I was he had come like a guest in quiet, to drink at
    my water-trough
And depart peaceful, pacified, and thankless,
Into the burning bowels of this earth?

Was it cowardice, that I dared not kill him?
Was it perversity that I longed to talk to him?
Was it humility, to feel honoured?
I felt so honoured.

And yet those voices:
If you were not afraid you would kill him.

And truly I was afraid, I was most afraid,
But even so, honoured still more
That he should seek my hospitality
From out the dark door of the secret earth.

He drank enough
And lifted his head, dreamily, as one who has drunken,
And flickered his tongue like a forked night on the air, so
      black,
Seeming to lick his lips,
And looked around like a god, unseeing, into the air,
And slowly turned his head,
And slowly, very slowly, as if thrice adream,
Proceeded to draw his slow length curving round
And climb again the broken bank of my wall-face.

And as he put his head into that dreadful hole,
And as he slowly drew up, snake-easing his shoulders, and
      entered further,
A sort of horror, a sort of protest against his withdrawing into
      that horrid black hole,
Deliberately going into the blackness, and slowly drawing
      himself after,
Overcame me now his back was turned.

I looked round, I put down my pitcher,
I picked up a clumsy log
And threw it at the water-trough with a clatter.

I think it did not hit him,
But suddenly that part of him that was left behind convulsed
     in undignified haste,
Writhed like lightning, and was gone
Into the black hole, the earth-lipped fissure in the wall-front,
At which, in the intense still noon, I stared with fascination.

And immediately I regretted it.
I thought how paltry, how vulgar, what a mean act!
I despised myself and the voices of my accursèd human educa·
     tion.
And I thought of the albatross,
And I wished he would come back, my snake.
For he seemed to me again like a king,
Like a king in exile, uncrowned in the underworld,
Now due to be crowned again.

And so, I missed my chance with one of the lords
Of life.
And I have something to expiate:
A pettiness.

D. H. LAWRENCE

THE SNAKE

A narrow fellow in the grass
Occasionally rides;
You may have met him, did you not?
His notice sudden is.

The grass divides as with a comb,
A spotted shaft is seen;
And then it closes at your feet
And opens farther on.

He likes a boggy acre,
A floor too cool for corn.
Yet when a boy, and barefoot,
I more than once, at noon,

Have passed, I thought, a whip-lash
Unbraiding in the sun,—
When, stooping to secure it,
It wrinkled, and was gone.

Several of nature's people
I know, and they know me;
I feel for them a transport
Of cordiality;

But never met this fellow,
Attended or alone,
Without a tighter breathing,
And zero at the bone.

EMILY DICKINSON

AN OTTER

Underwater eyes, an eel's
Oil of water body, neither fish nor beast is the otter:
Four-legged yet water-gifted, to outfish fish;
With webbed feet and long ruddering tail
And a round head like an old tomcat.

Brings the legend of himself
From before wars or burials, in spite of hounds and vermin-
poles;
Does not take root like the badger. Wanders, cries;
Gallops along land he no longer belongs to;
Re-enters the water by melting.

Of neither water nor land. Seeking
Some world lost when first he dived, that he cannot come at
since,
Takes his changed body into the holes of lakes;
As if blind, cleaves the stream's push till he licks
The pebbles of the source; from sea

To sea crosses in three nights
Like a king in hiding. Crying to the old shape of the starlit
land,
Over sunken farms where the bats go round,
Without answer. Till light and birdsong come
Walloping up roads with the milk wagon.

TED HUGHES

THE BULL

It is in captivity—
ringed, haltered, chained
to a drag
the bull is godlike

Unlike the cows
he lives alone, nozzles
the sweet grass gingerly
to pass the time away

He kneels, lies down
and stretching out
a foreleg licks himself
about the hoof

then stays
with half-closed eyes,
Olympian commentary on
the bright passage of days.

—The round sun
smooths his lacquer
through
the glossy pinetrees

his substance hard
as ivory or glass—
through which the wind
yet plays—
        milkless

he nods
the hair between his horns
and eyes matted
with hyacinthine curls.

WILLIAM CARLOS WILLIAMS

THE BULL CALF

The thing could barely stand. Yet taken
from his mother and the barn smells
he still impressed with his pride,
with the promise of sovereignty in the way
his head moved to take us in.
The fierce sunlight tugging the maize from the ground
licked at his shapely flanks.
He was too young for all that pride.
I thought of the deposed Richard II.

"No money in bull calves," Freeman had said.
The visiting clergyman rubbed the nostrils
now snuffing pathetically at the windless day.
"A pity," he sighed.
My gaze slipped off his hat toward the empty sky
that circled over the black knot of men,
over us and the calf waiting for the first blow.

Struck,
the bull calf drew in his thin forelegs
as if gathering strength for a mad rush . . .

tottered . . . raised his darkening eyes to us,
and I saw we were at the far end
of his frightened look, growing smaller and smaller
till we were only the ponderous mallet
that flicked his bleeding ear
and pushed him over on his side, stiffly,
like a block of wood.

Below the hill's crest
the river snuffled on the improvised beach.
We dug a deep pit and threw the dead calf into it.
It made a wet sound, a sepulchral gurgle,
as the warm sides bulged and flattened.
Settled, the bull calf lay as if asleep,
one foreleg over the other,
bereft of pride and so beautiful now,
without movement, perfectly still in the cool pit,
I turned away and wept.

IRVING LAYTON

Man's World

BLOW, BLOW, THOU WINTER WIND

Blow, blow, thou winter wind,
Thou art not so unkind
   As man's ingratitude;
Thy tooth is not so keen,
Because thou art not seen,
   Although thy breath be rude.
Heigh-ho! sing, heigh-ho! unto the green holly:
Most friendship is feigning, most loving mere folly:
   Then, heigh-ho, the holly!
   This life is most jolly.

Freeze, freeze, thou bitter sky,
That dost not bite so nigh
   As benefits forgot:
Though thou the waters warp,
Thy sting is not so sharp
   As friends remember'd not.
Heigh-ho! sing, heigh-ho! unto the green holly:
Most friendship is feigning, most loving mere folly:
   Then, heigh-ho, the holly!
   This life is most jolly.

WILLIAM SHAKESPEARE

THE HOLLOW MEN

A penny for the Old Guy

I

We are the hollow men
We are the stuffed men
Leaning together
Headpiece filled with straw. Alas!
Our dried voices, when
We whisper together
Are quiet and meaningless
As wind in dry grass
Or rats' feet over broken glass
In our dry cellar

Shape without form, shade without colour,
Paralyzed force, gesture without motion;

Those who have crossed
With direct eyes, to death's other Kingdom
Remember us—if at all—not as lost
Violent souls, but only
As the hollow men
The stuffed men.

II

Eyes I dare not meet in dreams
In death's dream kingdom
These do not appear:

There, the eyes are
Sunlight on a broken column

There, is a tree swinging
And voices are
In the wind's singing
More distant and more solemn
Than a fading star.

Let me be no nearer
In death's dream kingdom
Let me also wear
Such deliberate disguises
Rat's coat, crowskin, crossed staves
In a field
Behaving as the wind behaves
No nearer—

Not that final meeting
In the twilight kingdom.

III

This is the dead land
This is cactus land
Here the stone images
Are raised, here they receive
The supplication of a dead man's hand
Under the twinkle of a fading star.

Is it like this
In death's other kingdom
Waking alone
At the hour when we are
Trembling with tenderness
Lips that would kiss
Form prayers to broken stone.

IV

The eyes are not here
There are no eyes here
In this valley of dying stars
In this hollow valley
This broken jaw of our lost kingdoms

In this last of meeting places
We grope together
And avoid speech
Gathered on this beach of the tumid river

Sightless, unless
The eyes reappear
As the perpetual star
Multifoliate rose
Of death's twilight kingdom
The hope only
Of empty men.

V

Here we go round the prickly pear
Prickly pear prickly pear
Here we go round the prickly pear
At five o'clock in the morning.

Between the idea
And the reality
Between the motion

And the act
Falls the Shadow

For Thine is the Kingdom

Between the conception
And the creation
Between the emotion
And the response
Falls the Shadow
                    Life is very long

Between the desire
And the spasm
Between the potency
And the existence
Between the essence
And the descent
Falls the Shadow
                    For Thine is the Kingdom

For Thine is
Life is
For Thine is the

This is the way the world ends
This is the way the world ends
This is the way the world ends
Not with a bang but a whimper.

T. S. ELIOT

MOURNING'S AT EIGHT-THIRTY

or, A Headline a Day Keeps Euphoria Away

'Tis day. I waken, full of cheer,
   And cast the nightmare's shackle.
Hark, hark! the sanguine lark I hear
   Or possibly the grackle.

Phoebus arises. So do I;
   Then, tuneful from the shower,
Descend with head and courage high
   To greet the breakfast hour.

All's well with all my world. I seem
   A mover and a shaper
Till from the doorstep with the cream
   I fetch the morning paper—

Till I fetch in the paper and my hopes begin to bleed.
There's a famine on the Danube, there's a crisis on the Tweed,
And the foes of peace are clever,
And my bonds no good whatever,
And I wish I had never
   Learned to read.

The coffee curdling in my cup
   Turns bitterer than tonic,
For stocks are down and steaks are up
   And planes are supersonic.

Crops fail. Trains crash. The outlook's bright
   For none except the coffiner,
While empires topple left and right,
   Though Leftward rather oftener,

And Russia will not come to terms,
   And Sikhs are full of passion,
And each advertisement affirms
   My wardrobe's out of fashion.

Oh, I see by the papers we are dying by degrees.
There's a war upon our border, there's a blight upon our trees;
And to match each Wonder Drug up
That our scientists have dug up,
They have also turned the bug up
   Of a painful new disease.

At eventide the journals face
   In happier directions.
They like a juicy murder case,
   They dote on comic sections.

But in the morning even "Books"
   Sends shudders coursing through me.
The outlook for the Drama looks
   Intolerably gloomy,

And though the sun with all his heart
   Is shining round my shoulder,
I notice by the weather chart
   Tomorrow will be colder.

Oh, I wake in the dawning and my dreams are rosy-red,
But the papers all assure me there's destruction straight ahead.
If the present's pretty dismal,
Why, the future's quite abysmal,
And I think that I'll just
                    crawl
                            back
                                    to
                                        bed.

PHYLLIS McGINLEY

OZYMANDIAS

I met a traveller from an antique land
Who said: Two vast and trunkless legs of stone
Stand in the desert. Near them, on the sand,
Half sunk, a shattered visage lies, whose frown,
And wrinkled lip, and sneer of cold command,
Tell that its sculptor well those passions read
Which yet survive, stamped on these lifeless things,
The hand that mocked them, and the heart that fed:
And on the pedestal these words appear:
"My name is Ozymandias, King of Kings:
Look on my works, ye Mighty, and despair!"
Nothing beside remains. Round the decay
Of that colossal wreck, boundless and bare
The lone and level sands stretch far away.

PERCY BYSSHE SHELLEY

THE UNKNOWN CITIZEN

(To JS/07/M/378
This Marble Monument
Is Erected by the State)

He was found by the Bureau of Statistics to be
One against whom there was no official complaint,
And all the reports on his conduct agree
That, in the modern sense of an old-fashioned word, he was a
    saint,
For in everything he did he served the Greater Community.
Except for the War till the day he retired
He worked in a factory and never got fired,
But satisfied his employers, Fudge Motors Inc.
Yet he wasn't a scab or odd in his views,
For his Union reports that he paid his dues,
(Our report on his Union shows it was sound)
And our Social Psychology workers found
That he was popular with his mates and liked a drink.
The Press are convinced that he bought a paper every day
And that his reactions to advertisements were normal in every
    way.
Policies taken out in his name prove that he was fully insured,
And his Health-card shows he was once in hospital but left it
    cured.
Both Producers Research and High-Grade Living declare
He was fully sensible to the advantages of the Instalment Plan
And had everything necessary to the Modern Man,
A phonograph, a radio, a car and a frigidaire.
Our researchers into Public Opinion are content
That he held the proper opinions for the time of year;

When there was peace, he was for peace; when there was war,
　　he went.
He was married and added five children to the population,
Which our Eugenist says was the right number for a parent of
　　his generation,
And our teachers report that he never interfered with their
　　education.
Was he free? Was he happy? The question is absurd:
Had anything been wrong, we should certainly have heard.

W. H. AUDEN

ROLLER SKATE MAN

A freak of the city—
Little man with the big head
Shrivelled body, and stumps of legs
Based on a block of wood
Moving by roller-skate wheels.

On his hands gloves
Because the Queen Street pavements
Are rough when the hands are paddles
And he speeds between
The silk-stockinged legs
And the extravagant pleats:

Steering through familiar waters
Heavy with spit, old butts, chewed gum
Flotsam among the jetsam of this world.

RAYMOND SOUSTER

KINDLY UNHITCH THAT STAR, BUDDY

I hardly suppose I know anybody who wouldn't rather be a
success than a failure,
Just as I suppose every piece of crabgrass in the garden would
much rather be an azalea,
And in celestial circles all the run-of-the-mill angels would
rather be archangels or at least cherubim and seraphim,
And in the legal world all the little process-servers hope to
grow up into great big bailiffim and sheriffim.

Indeed, everybody wants to be a wow,
But not everybody knows exactly how.
Some people think they will eventually wear diamonds instead
of rhinestones
Only by everlastingly keeping their noses to their ghrinestones,
And other people think they will be able to put in more time
at Palm Beach and the Ritz
By not paying too much attention to attendance at the office
but rather in being brilliant by starts and fits.

Some people after a full day's work sit up all night getting a
college education by correspondence,
While others seem to think they'll get just as far by devoting
their evenings to the study of the difference in tempera-
ment between brunettance and blondance.
Some stake their all on luck,
And others put their faith in their ability to pass the buck.

In short, the world is filled with people trying to achieve success,
And half of them think they'll get it by saying No and half of
them by saying Yes,

And if all the ones who say No said Yes, and vice versa, such
   is the fate of humanity that ninety-nine per cent of them
   still wouldn't be any better off than they were before,
Which perhaps is just as well because if everybody was a success nobody could be contemptuous of anybody else and
   everybody would start in all over again trying to be a
   bigger success than everybody else so they would have
   somebody to be contemptuous of and so on forevermore,
Because when people start hitching their wagons to a star,
That's the way they are.

OGDEN NASH

THE STENOGRAPHERS

After the brief bivouac of Sunday,
their eyes, in the forced march of Monday to Saturday,
hoist the white flag, flutter in the snow storm of paper,
haul it down and crack in the midsun of temper.

In the pause between the first draft and the carbon
they glimpse the smooth hours when they were children—
the ride in the ice-cart, the ice-man's name,
the end of the route and the long walk home;

remember the sea where floats at high tide
were sea marrows growing on the scatter-green vine
or spools of grey toffee, or wasps' nests on water;
remember the sand and the leaves of the country.

Bell rings and they go and the voice draws their pencil
like a sled across snow; when its runners are frozen
rope snaps and the voice then is pulling no burden
but runs like a dog on the winter of paper.

Their climates are winter and summer—no wind
for the kites of their hearts—no wind for a flight;
a breeze at the most, to tumble them over
and leave them like rubbish—the boy-friends of blood.

In the inch of the noon as they move they are stagnant.
The terrible calm of the noon is their anguish;
the lip of the counter, the shapes of the straws
like icicles breaking their tongues are invaders.

Their beds are their oceans—salt water of weeping
the waves that they know—the tide before sleep;
and fighting to drown they assemble their sheep
in columns and watch them leap desks for their fences
and stare at them with their own mirror-worn faces.

In the felt of the morning the calico minded,
sufficiently starched, insert papers, hit keys,
efficient and sure as their adding machines;
yet they weep in the vault, they are taut as net curtains
stretched upon frames. In their eyes I have seen
the pin men of madness in marathon trim
race round the track of the stadium pupil.

P. K. PAGE

BLACK JACKETS

In the silence that prolongs the span
Rawly of music when the record ends,
   The red-haired boy who drove a van
In weekday overalls but, like his friends,

   Wore cycle boots and jacket here
To suit the Sunday hangout he was in,
   Heard, as he stretched back from his beer,
Leather creak softly round his neck and chin.

   Before him, on a coal-black sleeve
Remote exertion had lined, scratched, and burned
   Insignia that could not revive
The heroic fall or climb where they were earned.

   On the other drinkers bent together,
Concocting selves for their impervious kit,
   He saw it as no more than leather
Which, taut across the shoulders grown to it,

   Sent through the dimness of a bar
As sudden and anonymous hints of light
   As those that shipping give, that are
Now flickers in the Bay, now lost in night.

   He stretched out like a cat, and rolled
The bitterish taste of beer upon his tongue,
   And listened to a joke being told:
The present was the things he stayed among.

   If it was only loss he wore,
He wore it to assert, with fierce devotion,

Complicity and nothing more.
He recollected his initiation,

And one especially of the rites.
For on his shoulders they had put tattoos:
    The group's name on the left, The Knights,
And on the right the slogan Born To Lose.

THOM GUNN

DOWNTOWN CORNER NEWS STAND

It will need all of death to take you from this corner.
It has become your world, and you its unshaved
Bleary-eyed, foot-stamping king. In winter
You curse the cold, huddled in your coat from the wind,
You fry in summer like an egg hopping on a griddle,
And always the whining voice, the nervous-flinging arms,
The red face, the shifting eyes watching, waiting
Under the grimy cap for God knows what
To happen. (But nothing ever does; downtown
Toronto goes to sleep and wakes the next morning
Always the same, except a little dirtier.)
And you stand with your armful of Stars and Telys,
The peak of your cap well down against the sun,
And all the city's restless, seething river
Surges beside you, but not once do you plunge
Into its flood, or are carried or tossed away:
But reappear always, beard longer than ever, nose running,
To catch the noon editions at King and Bay.

RAYMOND SOUSTER

CHICAGO

Hog Butcher for the World,
Tool Maker, Stacker of Wheat,
Player with Railroads and the Nation's
    Freight Handler;
Stormy, husky, brawling,
City of the Big Shoulders:
They tell me you are wicked and I believe them, for I have
    seen your painted women under the gas lamps luring the
    farm boys.
And they tell me you are crooked and I answer: Yes, it is true
    I have seen the gunman kill and go free to kill again.

And they tell me you are brutal and my reply is: On the faces
    of women and children I have seen the marks of wanton
    hunger.
And having answered so, I turn once more to those who sneer
    at this my city, and I give them back the sneer and say to
    them:
Come and show me another city with lifted head singing so
    proud to be alive and coarse and strong and cunning.
Flinging magnetic curses amid the toil of piling job on job,
    here is a tall bold slugger set vivid against the little soft
    cities;
Fierce as a dog with tongue lapping for action, cunning as a
    savage pitted against the wilderness,
           Bareheaded,
           Shovelling,
           Wrecking,
           Planning,
           Building, breaking, rebuilding.
Under the smoke, dust all over his mouth, laughing with white
    teeth,

Under the terrible burden of destiny laughing as a young man
    laughs,
Laughing even as an ignorant fighter laughs who has never
    lost a battle,
Bragging and laughing that under his wrist is the pulse, and
    under his ribs the heart of the people,
              Laughing!

Laughing the stormy, husky, brawling laughter of Youth, half-
    naked, sweating, proud to be Hog Butcher, Tool Maker,
    Stacker of Wheat, Player with Railroads and Freight
    Handler to the Nation.

CARL SANDBURG

SUNK LYONESSE

In sea-cold Lyonesse,
When the Sabbath eve shafts down
On the roofs, walls, belfries
Of the foundered town,
The Nereids pluck their lyres
Where the green translucency beats,
And with motionless eyes at gaze
Make minstrelsy in the streets.
And the ocean water stirs
In salt-worn casemate and porch.
Plies the blunt-snouted fish
With fire in his skull for torch.
And the ringing wires resound;
And the unearthly lovely weep,

In lament of the music they make
In the sullen courts of sleep:
Whose marble flowers bloom for aye:
And—lapped by the moon-guiled tide—
Mock their carver with heart of stone,
Caged in his stone-ribbed side.

WALTER DE LA MARE

THE RAILROAD TRAIN

I like to see it lap the miles,
And lick the valleys up,
And stop to feed itself at tanks;
And then, prodigious, step

Around a pile of mountains,
And, supercilious, peer
In shanties by the sides of roads;
And then a quarry pare

To fit its sides
And crawl between
Complaining all the while
In horrid, hooting stanza;
Then chase itself down hill

And neigh like Boanerges;
Then, punctual as a star,
Stop—docile and omnipotent—
At its own stable door.

EMILY DICKINSON

THE EXPRESS

After the first powerful, plain manifesto
The black statement of pistons, without more fuss
But gliding like a queen, she leaves the station.
Without bowing and with restrained unconcern
She passes the houses which humbly crowd outside,
The gasworks and at last the heavy page
Of death, printed by gravestones in the cemetery.
Beyond the town, there lies the open country
Where, gathering speed, she acquires mystery,
The luminous self-possession of ships on ocean.
It is now she begins to sing—at first quite low
Then loud, and at last with a jazzy madness—
The song of her whistle screaming at curves,
Of deafening tunnels, brakes, innumerable bolts.
And always light, aerial, underneath,
Goes the elate metre of her wheels.
Steaming through metal landscape on her lines,
She plunges new eras of wild happiness
Where speed throws up strange shapes, broad curves
And parallels clean like trajectories from guns.
At last, further than Edinburgh or Rome,
Beyond the crest of the world, she reaches night
Where only a low streamline brightness
Of phosphorus on the tossing hills is light.
Ah, like a comet through flame, she moves entranced
Wrapt in her music no bird song, no, nor bough
Breaking with honey buds, shall ever equal.

STEPHEN SPENDER

TRAIN WINDOW

The dark green truck on the cement platform
is explicit as a paradigm.
Its wheels are four black cast-iron starfish.
Its body, a massive tray of planking,
ends in two close-set dark green uprights
crossed with three straight cross-pieces, one
looped with a white spiral of hose.

The truck holds eleven cakes of ice,
each cake a different size and shape.
Some look as though a weight had hit them.
One, solid glass, has a core of sugar.
They lean, a transitory Icehenge,
in a moor of imitation snow
from the hatchet's bright wet-sided steel.

Five galvanized pails, mottled, as if
of stiffened frosted caracul, three
with crescent lids and elbowed spouts,
loom in the ice, their half-hoop handles
linking that frozen elocution
to the running chalk-talk of powder-red
box-cars beyond, while our train waits here.

ROBERT FINCH

A THRENODY

"The new Rolls-Royce is designed to be owner driven. *No chauffeur required."*
—*From an advertisement in* The New Yorker.

Grandeur, farewell.
Farewell, pomp, glory, wealth's indulgent voice.
Tyre turned to dust in time. Great Carthage fell.
And owner-driven is the new Rolls-Royce.

Behold it, democratic front to back;
Nimble when traffic pinches;
Steered, braked by power; briefer than Cadillac
By eighteen inches;
Humming at sixty with an eerie purr
But needing no chauffeur.

What does it signify if radiator
(Altered but once, and that in '33,
When, at Sir Henry's death, or a little later,
The red R R was re-
Placed by a less conspicuous ebony)
Keeps still its ancient shape? What matter whether
The seats no minion now will ever use
Come padded in eight hides of English leather—
Enough for one hundred and twenty-eight pairs of shoes?
That the paint glistens and the brasses shine
More lusterful than hope?
That engineers have listened for axle-whine
With a stethoscope?

Splendour decays, despite the walnut table
Sliding from under the dash. Who now will stow

The wicker hampers away? For ladies in sable,
Who'll spread the cloth, uncork the Veuve Clicquot?
Who'll clean
The optional-special espresso coffee machine,
From folding bed whip off the cover of baize, or
Guard the electric razor?

Who but the owner-driver, squinting ahead
Through the marvellous glass, fretting when lights are red,
Studying on his lap
The cryptic, cross-marked, wife-defeating map?
He, it is he,
Tooling toward Cambridge, say (or Yale or Colgate),
On football afternoons, must nervously
Fumble for change at the tollgate,
Curse the careering drivers of both genders
Whose rods are hot,
Fear for his fourteen-times-enamelled fenders,
Search out the parking lot,
Remember the chains of winter, wrench the round wheel
Against the arrogant trucks, nor ever feel
Less mortal than man in Minx or Oldsmobile.

No one remains to touch a decorous forelock
Or fold a monogrammed blanket over the knees.
Gone the chauffeur—gone like Merlin the Warlock
And the unmourned chemise.
Gone newsboy's Grail, all that is rich and choice
And suave as David Niven.
Grandeur, a long farewell. The new Rolls-Royce
Is owner-driven.

PHYLLIS MCGINLEY

Religion

THE TYGER

TYGER! Tyger! burning bright
In the forests of the night,
What immortal hand or eye
Could frame thy fearful symmetry?

In what distant deeps or skies
Burnt the fire of thine eyes?
On what wings dare he aspire?
What the hand dare seize the fire?

And what shoulder, and what art,
Could twist the sinews of thy heart?
And when thy heart began to beat,
What dread hand? and what dread feet?

What the hammer? what the chain?
In what furnace was thy brain?
What the anvil? what dread grasp
Dare its deadly terrors clasp?

When the stars threw down their spears,
And water'd heaven with their tears,
Did he smile his work to see?
Did he who made the Lamb make thee?

Tyger! Tyger! burning bright
In the forests of the night,
What immortal hand or eye,
Dare frame thy fearful symmetry?

WILLIAM BLAKE

IN THE WILDERNESS

Christ of His gentleness
Thirsting and hungering,
Walked in the wilderness;
Soft words of grace He spoke
Unto lost desert-folk
That listened wondering.
He heard the bittern's call
From ruined palace wall,
Answered them brotherly.
He held communion
With the she-pelican
Of lonely piety.
Basilisk, cockatrice,
Flocked to His homilies,
With mail of dread device,
With monstrous barbèd stings,
With eager dragon-eyes;
Great rats on leather wings
And poor blind broken things,
Foul in their miseries.
And ever with Him went,
Of all His wanderings

Comrade, with ragged coat,
Gaunt ribs—poor innocent—
Bleeding foot, burning throat,
The guileless old scape-goat;
For forty nights and days
Followed in Jesus' ways,
Sure guard behind Him kept,
Tears like a lover wept.

ROBERT GRAVES

THE MAGI

Now as at all times I can see in the mind's eye,
In their stiff, painted clothes, the pale unsatisfied ones
Appear and disappear in the blue depth of the sky
With all their ancient faces like rain-beaten stones,
And all their helms of silver hovering side by side,
And all their eyes still fixed, hoping to find once more,
Being by Calvary's turbulence unsatisfied,
The uncontrollable mystery on the bestial floor.

WILLIAM BUTLER YEATS

JOURNEY OF THE MAGI

"A cold coming we had of it,
Just the worst time of the year
For a journey, and such a long journey:
The ways deep and the weather sharp,

The very dead of winter."
And the camels galled, sore-footed, refractory,
Lying down in the melting snow.
There were times we regretted
The summer palaces on slopes, the terraces,
And the silken girls bringing sherbet.
Then the camel men cursing and grumbling
And running away, and wanting their liquor and women,
And the night-fires going out, and the lack of shelters,
And the cities hostile and the towns unfriendly
And the villages dirty and charging high prices:
A hard time we had of it.
At the end we preferred to travel all night,
Sleeping in snatches,
With the voices singing in our ears, saying
That this was all folly.

Then at dawn we came down to a temperate valley,
Wet, below the snow line, smelling of vegetation;
With a running stream and a water-mill beating the darkness,
And three trees on the low sky,
And an old white horse galloped away in the meadow.
Then we came to a tavern with vine-leaves over the lintel,
Six hands at an open door dicing for pieces of silver,
And feet kicking the empty wine-skins.
But there was no information, and so we continued
And arrived at evening, not a moment too soon
Finding the place; it was (you may say) satisfactory.

All this was a long time ago, I remember,
And I would do it again, but set down
This set down
This: were we led all that way for

Birth or Death? There was a Birth, certainly,
We had evidence and no doubt. I had seen birth and death,
But had thought they were different; this Birth was
Hard and bitter agony for us, like Death, our death.
We returned to our places, these Kingdoms,
But no longer at ease here, in the old dispensation,
With an alien people clutching their gods.
I should be glad of another death.

T. S. ELIOT

Art

TO A POET A THOUSAND YEARS HENCE

I who am dead a thousand years,
    And wrote this sweet archaic song,
Send you my words for messengers
    The way I shall not pass along.

I care not if you bridge the seas,
    Or ride secure the cruel sky,
Or build consummate palaces
    Of metal or of masonry.

But have you wine and music still,
    And statues and a bright-eyed love,
And foolish thoughts of good and ill,
    And prayers to them who sit above?

How shall we conquer? Like a wind
    That falls at eve our fancies blow,
And old Maeonides the blind
    Said it three thousand years ago.

O friend unseen, unborn, unknown,
    Student of our sweet English tongue,
Read out my words at night, alone:
    I was a poet, I was young.

Since I can never see your face,
    And never shake you by the hand,
I send my soul through time and space
    To greet you. You will understand.

JAMES ELROY FLECKER

THE SOLITARY REAPER

Behold her, single in the field,
Yon solitary highland lass!
Reaping and singing by herself;
Stop here, or gently pass!
Alone she cuts and binds the grain,
And sings a melancholy strain;
O, listen! for the vale profound
Is overflowing with the sound.

No nightingale did ever chaunt
More welcome notes to weary bands
Of travellers in some shady haunt
Among Arabian sands:
A voice so thrilling ne'er was heard
In spring-time from the cuckoo-bird,
Breaking the silence of the seas
Among the farthest Hebrides.

Will no one tell me what she sings?—
Perhaps the plaintive numbers flow
For old, unhappy, far-off things,
And battles long ago.

Or is it some more humble lay,
Familiar matter of today?
Some natural sorrow, loss, or pain,
That has been, and may be again?

Whate'er the theme, the maiden sang
As if her song could have no ending;
I saw her singing at her work,
And o'er the sickle bending;—
I listened, motionless and still;
And, as I mounted up the hill,
The music in my heart I bore,
Long after it was heard no more.

WILLIAM WORDSWORTH

KUBLA KHAN

In Xanadu did Kubla Khan
A stately pleasure-dome decree:
Where Alph, the sacred river, ran
Through caverns measureless to man
      Down to a sunless sea.
So twice five miles of fertile ground
With walls and towers were girdled round:
And there were gardens bright with sinuous rills,
Where blossomed many an incense-bearing tree;
And here were forests ancient as the hills,
Enfolding sunny spots of greenery.

But oh! that deep romantic chasm which slanted
Down the green hill athwart a cedarn cover!

A savage place! as holy and enchanted
As e'er beneath a waning moon was haunted
By woman wailing for her demon-lover!
And from this chasm, with ceaseless turmoil seething,
As if this earth in fast thick pants were breathing,
A mighty fountain momently was forced:
Amid whose swift half-intermitted burst
Huge fragments vaulted like rebounding hail,
Or chaffy grain beneath the thresher's flail:
And 'mid these dancing rocks at once and ever
It flung up momently the sacred river.
Five miles meandering with a mazy motion
Through wood and dale the sacred river ran,
Then reached the caverns measureless to man,
And sank in tumult to a lifeless ocean:
And 'mid this tumult Kubla heard from far
Ancestral voices prophesying war!
      The shadow of the dome of pleasure
      Floated midway on the waves;
      Where was heard the mingled measure
      From the fountain and the caves.
It was a miracle of rare device,
A sunny pleasure-dome with caves of ice!

      A damsel with a dulcimer
      In a vision once I saw:
      It was an Abyssinian maid,
      And on her dulcimer she played,
      Singing of Mount Abora.
      Could I revive within me
      Her symphony and song,
      To such a deep delight 'twould win me,
That with music loud and long,

I would build that dome in air,
That sunny dome! those caves of ice!
And all who heard should see them there,
And all should cry, Beware! Beware!
His flashing eyes, his floating hair!
Weave a circle round him thrice,
And close your eyes with holy dread,
For he on honey-dew hath fed,
And drunk the milk of Paradise.

SAMUEL TAYLOR COLERIDGE

THE MAN WITH THE BLUE GUITAR

I

The man bent over his guitar,
A shearsman of sorts. The day was green.

They said, "You have a blue guitar,
You do not play things as they are."

The man replied, "Things as they are
Are changed upon the blue guitar."

And they said then, "But play, you must,
A tune beyond us, yet ourselves,

A tune upon the blue guitar
Of things exactly as they are."

II

I cannot bring a world quite round,
Although I patch it as I can.

I sing a hero's head, large eye
And bearded bronze, but not a man,

Although I patch him as I can
And reach through him almost to man.

If to serenade almost to man
Is to miss, by that, things as they are,

Say that it is the serenade
Of a man that plays a blue guitar.

WALLACE STEVENS

Form and Language
in Poetry

Poetic Forms

RICHARD CORY

Whenever Richard Cory went down town,
 We people on the pavement looked at him:
He was a gentleman from sole to crown,
 Clean favoured, and imperially slim.

And he was always quietly arrayed,
 And he was always human when he talked;
But still he fluttered pulses when he said,
 "Good-morning," and he glittered when he walked.

And he was rich—yes, richer than a king—
 And admirably schooled in every grace:
In fine, we thought that he was everything
 To make us wish that we were in his place.

So on we worked, and waited for the light,
 And went without the meat, and cursed the bread;
And Richard Cory, one calm summer night,
 Went home and put a bullet through his head.

EDWIN ARLINGTON ROBINSON

THE LADY OF SHALOTT

I

On either side the river lie
Long fields of barley and of rye,
That clothe the wold and meet the sky;
And thro' the field the road runs by
       To many-tower'd Camelot;
And up and down the people go,
Gazing where the lilies blow
Round an island there below,
       The island of Shalott.

Willows whiten, aspens quiver,
Little breezes dusk and shiver
Thro' the wave that runs for ever
By the island in the river
       Flowing down to Camelot.
Four grey walls, and four grey towers,
Overlook a space of flowers,
And the silent isle imbowers
       The Lady of Shalott.

By the margin, willow-veil'd,
Slide the heavy barges trail'd
By slow horses; and unhail'd
The shallop flitteth silken-sail'd
       Skimming down to Camelot:
But who hath seen her wave her hand?
Or at the casement seen her stand?
Or is she known in all the land,
       The Lady of Shalott?

Only reapers, reaping early
In among the bearded barley,
Hear a song that echoes cheerly
From the river winding clearly,
  Down to tower'd Camelot:
And by the moon the reaper weary,
Piling sheaves in uplands airy,
Listening, whispers, "'Tis the fairy
  Lady of Shalott."

II

There she weaves by night and day
A magic web with colours gay.
She has heard a whisper say,
A curse is on her if she stay
  To look down to Camelot.
She knows not what the curse may be,
And so she weaveth steadily,
And little other care hath she,
  The Lady of Shalott.

And moving thro' a mirror clear
That hangs before her all the year,
Shadows of the world appear.
There she sees the highway near
  Winding down to Camelot:
There the river eddy whirls,
And there the surly village-churls,
And the red cloaks of market girls,
  Pass onward from Shalott.

Sometimes a troop of damsels glad,
An abbot on an ambling pad,

Sometimes a curly shepherd-lad,
Or long-hair'd page in crimson clad,
      Goes by to tower'd Camelot;
And sometimes thro' the mirror blue
The knights come riding two and two:
She hath no loyal knight and true,
      The Lady of Shalott.

But in her web she still delights
To weave the mirror's magic sights,
For often thro' the silent nights
A funeral, with plumes and lights,
      And music, went to Camelot:
Or when the moon was overhead,
Came two young lovers lately wed;
"I am half sick of shadows," said
      The Lady of Shalott.

III

A bow-shot from her bower-eaves,
He rode between the barley-sheaves,
The sun came dazzling thro' the leaves,
And flamed upon the brazen greaves
      Of bold Sir Lancelot.
A red-cross knight for ever kneel'd
To a lady in his shield,
That sparkled on the yellow field,
      Beside remote Shalott.

The gemmy bridle glitter'd free,
Like to some branch of stars we see

Hung in the golden galaxy.
The bridle bells rang merrily
        As he rode down to Camelot:
And from his blazon'd baldric slung
A mighty silver bugle hung,
And as he rode his armour rung,
        Beside remote Shalott.

All in the blue unclouded weather
Thick-jewell'd shone the saddle-leather,
The helmet and the helmet-feather
Burn'd like one burning flame together,
        As he rode down to Camelot.
As often thro' the purple night,
Below the starry clusters bright,
Some bearded meteor, trailing light,
        Moves over still Shalott.

His broad clear brow in sunlight glow'd;
On burnish'd hooves his war-horse trode;
From underneath his helmet flow'd
His coal-black curls as on he rode,
        As he rode down to Camelot.
From the bank and from the river
He flash'd into the crystal mirror,
"Tirra lirra," by the river
        Sang Sir Lancelot.

She left the web, she left the loom,
She made three paces thro' the room,
She saw the water-lily bloom,
She saw the helmet and the plume,
        She look'd down to Camelot.

Out flew the web and floated wide;
The mirror crack'd from side to side;
"The curse is come upon me," cried
      The Lady of Shalott.

IV

In the stormy east-wind straining,
The pale yellow woods were waning,
The broad stream in his banks complaining,
Heavily the low sky raining
      Over tower'd Camelot;
Down she came and found a boat
Beneath a willow left afloat,
And round about the prow she wrote
      The Lady of Shalott.

And down the river's dim expanse—
Like some bold seer in a trance,
Seeing all his own mischance—
With a glassy countenance
      Did she look to Camelot.
And at the closing of the day
She loosed the chain, and down she lay;
The broad stream bore her far away,
      The Lady of Shalott.

Lying, robed in snowy white
That loosely flew to left and right—
The leaves upon her falling light—
Thro' the noises of the night
      She floated down to Camelot:
And as the boat-head wound along
The willowy hills and fields among,

They heard her singing her last song,
      The Lady of Shalott.

Heard a carol, mournful, holy,
Chanted loudly, chanted lowly,
Till her blood was frozen slowly,
And her eyes were darken'd wholly,
      Turn'd to tower'd Camelot.
For ere she reach'd upon the tide
The first house by the water-side,
Singing in her song she died,
      The Lady of Shalott.

Under tower and balcony,
By garden-wall and gallery,
A gleaming shape she floated by,
Dead-pale between the houses high,
      Silent into Camelot.
Out upon the wharfs they came,
Knight and burgher, lord and dame,
And round the prow they read her name,
      The Lady of Shalott.

Who is this? and what is here?
And in the lighted palace near
Died the sound of royal cheer;
And they cross'd themselves for fear,
      All the knights at Camelot:
But Lancelot mused a little space;
He said, "She has a lovely face;
God in his mercy lend her grace,
      The Lady of Shalott."

ALFRED LORD TENNYSON

MY LAST DUCHESS

That's my last Duchess painted on the wall,
Looking as if she were alive. I call
That piece a wonder, now; Fra Pandolf's hands
Worked busily a day, and there she stands.
Will't please you sit and look at her? I said
"Fra Pandolf" by design, for never read
Strangers like you that pictured countenance,
The depth and passion of its earnest glance,
But to myself they turned (since none puts by
The curtain I have drawn for you, but I)
And seemed as they would ask me, if they durst,
How such a glance came there; so, not the first
Are you to turn and ask thus. Sir, 'twas not
Her husband's presence only, called that spot
Of joy into the Duchess' cheek: perhaps
Fra Pandolf chanced to say, "Her mantle laps
Over my lady's wrist too much," or "Paint
Must never hope to reproduce the faint
Half-flush that dies along her throat"; such stuff
Was courtesy, she thought, and cause enough
For calling up that spot of joy. She had
A heart—how shall I say?—too soon made glad,
Too easily impressed; she liked whate'er
She looked on, and her looks went everywhere.

Sir, 'twas all one! My favour at her breast,
The dropping of the daylight in the west,
The bough of cherries some officious fool
Broke in the orchard for her, the white mule
She rode with round the terrace—all and each
Would draw from her alike the approving speech,

Or blush, at least. She thanked men,—good; but thanked
Somehow—I know not how—as if she ranked
My gift of a nine-hundred-year's-old name
With anybody's gift. Who'd stoop to blame
This sort of trifling? Even had you skill
In speech—(which I have not)—to make your will
Quite clear to such an one, and say, "Just this
Or that in you disgusts me; here you miss,
Or there exceed the mark"—and if she let
Herself be lessoned so, nor plainly set
Her wits to yours, forsooth, and made excuse,
—E'en then would be some stooping; and I choose
Never to stoop.

              Oh, sir, she smiled, no doubt,
Whene'er I passed her; but who passed without
Much the same smile? This grew; I gave commands;
Then all smiles stopped together. There she stands
As if alive. Will't please you rise? We'll meet
The company below, then. I repeat,
The Count your master's known munificence
Is ample warrant that no just pretence
Of mine for dowry will be disallowed;
Though his fair daughter's self, as I avowed
At starting, is my object. Nay, we'll go
Together down, sir! Notice Neptune, though,
Taming a sea-horse, thought a rarity,
Which Claus of Innsbruck cast in bronze for me!

                           Robert Browning

SHALL I COMPARE THEE

Shall I compare thee to a summer's day? *a*
Thou art more lovely and more temperate; *b*
Rough winds do shake the darling buds of May, *a*
And summer's lease hath all too short a date: *b*
Sometime too hot the eye of heaven shines, *c*
And often is his gold complexion dimm'd; *d*
And every fair from fair sometime declines, *c*
By chance, or nature's changing course, untrimm'd; *d*
But thy eternal summer shall not fade, *e*
Nor lose possession of that fair thou ow'st, *f*
Nor shall Death brag thou wander'st in his shade, *e*
When in eternal lines to time thou grow'st. *f*
    So long as men can breathe, or eyes can see, *g*
    So long lives this, and this gives life to thee. *g*

WILLIAM SHAKESPEARE

THE WORLD IS TOO MUCH WITH US

The world is too much with us; late and soon,
Getting and spending, we lay waste our powers:
Little we see in nature that is ours;
We have given our hearts away, a sordid boon!
This sea that bares her bosom to the moon;
The winds that will be howling at all hours,
And are up-gathered now like sleeping flowers;
For this, for everything, we are out of tune;

It moves us not.—Great God! I'd rather be
A pagan suckled in a creed outworn;
So might I, standing on this pleasant lea,
Have glimpses that would make me less forlorn;
Have sight of Proteus rising from the sea;
Or hear old Triton blow his wreathèd horn.

WILLIAM WORDSWORTH

ON HIS BLINDNESS

When I consider how my light is spent
Ere half my days, in this dark world and wide,
And that one talent which is death to hide
Lodged with me useless, though my soul more bent
To serve therewith my Maker, and present
My true account, lest He returning chide,
"Doth God exact day-labour, light denied?"
I fondly ask; but Patience, to prevent
That murmur, soon replies: "God doth not need
Either man's work, or His own gifts; who best
Bear His mild yoke, they serve Him best. His state
Is kingly; thousands at His bidding speed,
And post o'er land and ocean without rest;—
They also serve who only stand and wait."

JOHN MILTON

NEXT TO OF COURSE GOD

"next to of course god america i
love you land of the pilgrims' and so forth oh
say can you see by the dawn's early my
country 'tis of centuries come and go
and are no more what of it we should worry
in every language even deafanddumb
thy sons acclaim your glorious name by gorry
by jingo by gee by gosh by gum
why talk of beauty what could be more beautiful than these heroic happy dead
who rushed like lions to the roaring slaughter
they did not stop to think they died instead
then shall the voice of liberty be mute?"

He spoke.   And drank rapidly a glass of water

E. E. CUMMINGS

ODE TO AUTUMN

Season of mists and mellow fruitfulness,
    Close bosom-friend of the maturing sun;
Conspiring with him how to load and bless
    With fruit the vines that round the thatch-eaves run;
To bend with apples the moss'd cottage-trees,
    And fill all fruit with ripeness to the core;
        To swell the gourd, and plump the hazel shells

With a sweet kernel; to set budding more
  And still more, later flowers for the bees,
  Until they think warm days will never cease;
    For Summer has o'erbrimm'd their clammy cells.

Who hath not seen thee oft amid thy store?
  Sometimes whoever seeks abroad may find
Thee sitting careless on a granary floor,
  Thy hair soft-lifted by the winnowing wind;
Or on a half-reap'd furrow sound asleep,
  Drowsed with the fume of poppies, while thy hook
    Spares the next swath and all its twinèd flowers;
And sometimes like a gleaner thou dost keep
  Steady thy laden head across a brook;
  Or by a cider-press, with patient look,
    Thou watchest the last oozings, hour by hour.

Where are the songs of Spring? Ay, where are they?
  Think not of them,—thou hast thy music too,
While barrèd clouds bloom the soft-dying day,
  And touch the stubble-plains with rosy hue;
Then in a wailful choir the small gnats mourn
  Among the river-sallows, borne aloft
    Or sinking as the light wind lives or dies;
And full-grown lambs loud bleat from hilly bourn;
  Hedge-crickets sing; and now with treble soft
  The redbreast whistles from a garden croft:
    And gathering swallows twitter in the skies.

JOHN KEATS

ELEGY WRITTEN IN A COUNTRY CHURCHYARD

The curfew tolls the knell of parting day,
The lowing herd wind slowly o'er the lea,
The plowman homeward plods his weary way,
And leaves the world to darkness and to me.

Now fades the glimmering landscape on the sight,
And all the air a solemn stillness holds,
Save where the beetle wheels his droning flight,
And drowsy tinklings lull the distant folds;

Save that from yonder ivy-mantled tow'r
The moping owl does to the moon complain
Of such, as wand'ring near her secret bow'r,
Molest her ancient solitary reign.

Beneath those rugged elms, that yew-tree's shade,
Where heaves the turf in many a mould'ring heap,
Each in his narrow cell for ever laid,
The rude forefathers of the hamlet sleep.

The breezy call of incense-breathing morn,
The swallow twitt'ring from the straw-built shed,
The cock's shrill clarion, or the echoing horn,
No more shall rouse them from their lowly bed.

For them no more the blazing hearth shall burn,
Or busy housewife ply her evening care:
No children run to lisp their sire's return,
Or climb his knees the envied kiss to share.

Oft did the harvest to their sickle yield,
Their furrow oft the stubborn glebe has broke;
How jocund did they drive their team afield!
How bow'd the woods beneath their sturdy stroke!

Let not Ambition mock their useful toil,
Their homely joys, and destiny obscure;
Nor Grandeur hear with a disdainful smile,
The short and simple annals of the poor.

The boast of heraldry, the pomp of pow'r,
And all that beauty, all that wealth e'er gave,
Awaits alike th' inevitable hour.
The paths of glory lead but to the grave.

Nor you, ye proud, impute to these the fault,
If Mem'ry o'er their tomb no trophies raise,
Where thro' the long-drawn aisle and fretted vault
The pealing anthem swells the note of praise.

Can storied urn or animated bust
Back to its mansion call the fleeting breath?
Can Honour's voice provoke the silent dust,
Or Flatt'ry sooth the dull cold ear of Death?

Perhaps in this neglected spot is laid
Some heart once pregnant with celestial fire;
Hands, that the rod of empire might have sway'd,
Or wak'd to ecstasy the living lyre.

But Knowledge to their eyes her ample page
Rich with the spoils of time did ne'er unroll;
Chill Penury repress'd their noble rage,
And froze the genial current of the soul.

Full many a gem of purest ray serene,
The dark unfathom'd caves of ocean bear:
Full many a flower is born to blush unseen,
And waste its sweetness on the desert air.

Some village Hampden, that with dauntless breast
The little tyrant of his fields withstood;
Some mute inglorious Milton here may rest,
Some Cromwell guiltless of his country's blood.

Th' applause of list'ning senates to command,
The threats of pain and ruin to despise,
To scatter plenty o'er a smiling land,
And read their hist'ry in a nation's eyes,

Their lot forbade; nor circumscrib'd alone
Their growing virtues, but their crimes confin'd;
Forbade to wade through slaughter to a throne,
And shut the gates of mercy on mankind,

The struggling pangs of conscious truth to hide,
To quench the blushes of ingenuous shame,
Or heap the shrine of Luxury and Pride
With incense kindled at the Muse's flame.

Far from the madding crowd's ignoble strife,
Their sober wishes never learn'd to stray;
Along the cool sequester'd vale of life
They kept the noiseless tenor of their way.

Yet ev'n these bones from insult to protect
Some frail memorial still erected nigh,
With uncouth rhymes and shapeless sculpture deck'd,
Implores the passing tribute of a sigh.

Their name, their years, spelt by th' unletter'd muse,
The place of fame and elegy supply:
And many a holy text around she strews,
That teach the rustic moralist to die.

For who, to dumb Forgetfulness a prey,
This pleasing anxious being e'er resign'd,
Left the warm precincts of the cheerful day,
Nor cast one longing ling'ring look behind?

On some fond breast the parting soul relies,
Some pious drops the closing eye requires;
Ev'n from the tomb the voice of Nature cries,
Ev'n in our ashes live their wonted fires.

For thee, who mindful of th' unhonour'd dead
Dost in these lines their artless tale relate;
If chance, by lonely contemplation led,
Some kindred spirit shall inquire thy fate,

Haply some hoary-headed swain may say,
"Oft have we seen him at the peep of dawn
Brushing with hasty steps the dews away
To meet the sun upon the upland lawn.

"There at the foot of yonder nodding beech
That wreathes its old fantastic roots so high,
His listless length at noontide would he stretch,
And pore upon the brook that babbles by.

"Hard by yon wood, now smiling as in scorn,
Mutt'ring his wayward fancies he would rove,
Now drooping, woeful wan, like one forlorn,
Or craz'd with care, or cross'd in hopeless love.

"One morn I miss'd him on the custom'd hill,
Along the heath and near his fav'rite tree;
Another came; nor yet beside the rill,
Nor up the lawn, nor at the wood was he;

"The next with dirges due in sad array
Slow thro' the church-way path we saw him borne.
Approach and read (for thou can'st read) the lay,
Grav'd on the stone beneath yon aged thorn."

THE EPITAPH

Here rests his head upon the lap of Earth
A youth to Fortune and to Fame unknown.
Fair Science frown'd not on his humble birth,
And Melancholy mark'd him for her own.

Large was his bounty, and his soul sincere,
Heav'n did a recompense as largely send:
He gave to Mis'ry all he had, a tear,
He gain'd from Heav'n ('twas all he wish'd) a friend.

No farther seek his merits to disclose,
Or draw his frailties from their dread abode,
(There they alike in trembling hope repose,)
The bosom of his Father and his God.

THOMAS GRAY

HUMMING-BIRD

I can imagine, in some otherworld
Primeval-dumb, far back
In that most awful stillness, that only gasped and hummed,
Humming-birds raced down the avenues.

Before anything had a soul,
While life was a heave of Matter, half inanimate,
This little bit chipped off in brilliance
And went whizzing through the slow, vast succulent stems.

I believe there were no flowers then,
In the world where the humming-bird flashed ahead of creation.
I believe he pierced the slow vegetable veins with his long beak.
Probably he was big
As mosses, and little lizards, they say, were once big.
Probably he was a jabbing, terrifying monster.

We look at him through the wrong end of the long telescope of
      Time.
Luckily for us.

                                        D. H. LAWRENCE

JUST AS I USED TO SAY

         Just as I used to say
                        love comes harder to the aged
because they've been running
                  on the same old rails too long
   and then when the sly switch comes along
                              they miss the turn

160

and burn up the wrong rail while
                          the gay caboose goes flying
          and the steamengine driver don't recognize
                          them new electric horns
and the aged run out on the rusty spur
                          which ends up in
              the dead grass where
     ·the rusty tincans and bedsprings and old razor
              blades and moldy mattresses
                          lie
          and the rail breaks off dead
                          right there
          though the ties go on awhile
                          and the aged
say to themselves
              Well
                     this must be the place
              we were supposed to lie down
     And they do
              while the bright saloon careens along away
     on a high
          hilltop
                     its windows full of bluesky and lovers
          with flowers
                     their long hair streaming
                          and all of them laughing
              and waving and
                     whispering to each other
          and looking out and
                     wondering what that graveyard
          where the rails end
                     is

Lawrence Ferlinghetti

Poetic Language

THE LAKE ISLE OF INNISFREE

I will arise and go now, and go to Innisfree,
And a small cabin build there, of clay and wattles made:
Nine bean-rows will I have there, a hive for the honey-bee,
And live alone in the bee-loud glade.

And I shall have some peace there, for peace comes dropping
    slow,
Dropping from the veils of the morning to where the cricket
    sings;
There midnight's all a glimmer, and noon a purple glow,
And evening full of the linnet's wings.

I will arise and go now, for always night and day
I hear lake water lapping with low sounds by the shore;
While I stand on the roadway, or on the pavements grey,
I hear it in the deep heart's core.

WILLIAM BUTLER YEATS

THE KALLYOPE YELL

I

Proud men
Eternally
Go about
Slander me,
Call me the "Calliope,"
Sizz . . .
Fizz . . .

II

I am the Gutter Dream,
Tune-maker, born of steam,
Tooting joy, tooting hope.
I am the Kallyope.
Car called the Kallyope.
Willy willy willy wah HOO!
See the flags: snow-white tent,
See the bear and elephant,
See the monkey jump the rope,
Listen to the Kallyope, Kallyope, Kallyope!
Soul of the rhinoceros
And the hippopotamus
(Listen to the lion roar!)
Jaguar, cockatoot,
Loons, owls,
Hoot, hoot.
Listen to the lion roar,
Listen to the lion roar,
Listen to the lion R-O-A-R!
Hear the leopard cry for gore,
Willy willy willy wah HOO!

Hail the bloody Indian band,
Hail, all hail the popcorn stand,
Hail to Barnum's picture there,
People's idol everywhere,
Whoop whoop whoop WHOOP!
Music of the mob am I,
Circus day's tremendous cry:—
I am the Kallyope, Kallyope, Kallyope!
Hoot toot, hoot toot, hoot toot, hoot toot,
Willy willy willy wah HOO!
Sizz, fizz. . . .

III

Born of mobs, born of steam,
Listen to my golden dream,
Listen to my golden dream,
Listen to my G-O-L-D-E-N D-R-E-A-M!
Whoop whoop whoop whoop WHOOP!
I will blow the proud folk low,
Humanize the dour and slow,
I will shake the proud folk down,
(Listen to the lion roar!)
Popcorn crowds shall rule the town—
Willy willy willy wah HOO!
Steam shall work melodiously,
Brotherhood increase.
You'll see the world and all it holds
For fifty cents apiece.
Willy willy willy wah HOO!
Every day a circus day.

What?

Well, almost every day.
Nevermore the sweater's den,
Nevermore the prison pen.
Gone the war on land and sea
That aforetime troubled men.
Nations all in amity,
Happy in their plumes arrayed
In the long bright street parade.
Bands a-playing every day.

What?

Well, almost every day.
I am the Kallyope, Kallyope, Kallyope!
Willy, willy, willy, wah HOO!
Hoot toot, hoot toot,
Whoop whoop whoop whoop,
Willy willy willy wah HOO!
Sizz, fizz. . . .

IV

Every soul
Resident
In the earth's one circus-tent!
Every man a trapeze king,
Then a pleased spectator there.
On the benches! In the ring!
While the neighbours gawk and stare
And the cheering rolls along.
Almost every day a race
When the merry starting gong
Rings, each chariot on the line,
Every driver fit and fine
With a steel-spring Roman grace.

Almost every day a dream,
Almost every day a dream.
Every girl,
Maid or wife,
Wild with music,
Eyes agleam
With that marvel called desire:
Actress, princess, fit for life,
Armed with honour like a knife,
Jumping thro' the hoops of fire.
(Listen to the lion roar!)
Making all the children shout.
Clowns shall tumble all about,
Painted high and full of song
While the cheering rolls along,
Tho' they scream,
Tho' they rage,
Every beast
In his cage,
Every beast
In his den
That aforetime troubled men.

V

I am the Kallyope, Kallyope, Kallyope,
Tooting hope, tooting hope, tooting hope, tooting hope;
Shaking window-pane and door
With a crashing cosmic tune,
With the war-cry of the spheres,
Rhythm of the roar of noon,
Rhythm of Niagara's roar,
Voicing planet, star and moon,
Shrieking of the better years.

Prophet-singers will arise,
Prophets coming after me,
Sing my song in softer guise
With more delicate surprise;
I am but the pioneer
Voice of Democracy;
I am the gutter dream,
I am the golden dream,
Singing science, singing steam.
I will blow the proud folk down,
(Listen to the lion roar!)
I am the Kallyope, Kallyope, Kallyope,
Tooting hope, tooting hope, tooting hope, tooting hope,
Willy willy willy wah HOO!
Hoot toot, hoot toot, hoot toot, hoot toot,
Whoop whoop, whoop whoop,
Whoop whoop, whoop whoop,
Willy willy willy wah HOO!
Sizz . . .
Fizz . . .

VACHEL LINDSAY

THE WEARY BLUES

Droning a drowsy syncopated tune,
Rocking back and forth to a mellow croon,
    I heard a Negro play.
Down on Lenox Avenue the other night
By the pale dull pallor of an old gas light
    He did a lazy sway. . . .
    He did a lazy sway. . . .

To the tune o' those Weary Blues.
With his ebony hands on each ivory key
He made that poor piano moan with melody.
O Blues!

Swaying to and fro on his rickety stool
He played that sad raggy tune like a musical fool.
Sweet Blues!
Coming from a black man's soul.
O Blues!

In a deep song voice with a melancholy tone
I heard that Negro sing, that old piano moan—
"Ain't got nobody in all this world,
Ain't got nobody but maself.
I's gwine to quit ma frownin'
And put ma troubles on the shelf."
Thump, thump, thump, went his foot on the floor.
He played a few chords then he sang some more—

"I got the Weary Blues
And I can't be satisfied.
Got the Weary Blues
And can't be satisfied—
I ain't happy no mo'
And I wish that I had died."

And far into the night he crooned that tune.
The stars went out and so did the moon.
The singer stopped playing and went to bed
While the Weary Blues echoed through his head.
He slept like a rock or a man that's dead.

LANGSTON HUGHES

A HYMN TO GOD THE FATHER

Wilt Thou forgive that sin where I begun,
 Which is my sin, though it were done before?
Wilt Thou forgive those sins, through which I run,
 And do run still: though still I do deplore?
  When Thou hast done, Thou hast not done,
   For I have more.

With Thou forgive that sin by which I've won
 Others to sin? and, made my sin their door?
Wilt Thou forgive that sin which I did shun
 A year, or two: but wallowed in, a score?
  When Thou hast done, Thou hast not done,
   For I have more.

I have a sin of fear, that when I have spun
 My last thread, I shall perish on the shore;
Swear by Thy self, that at my death Thy son
 Shall shine as he shines now, and heretofore;
  And, having done that, Thou hast done,
   I fear no more.

JOHN DONNE

THE GREAT LOVER

I have been so great a lover: filled my days
So proudly with the splendour of love's praise,
The pain, the calm, and the astonishment,
Desire illimitable, and still content,

And all dear names men use, to cheat despair,
For the perplexed and viewless streams that bear
Our hearts at random down the dark of life.
Now, ere the unthinking silence on that strife
Steals down, I would cheat drowsy death so far,
My night shall be remembered for a star
That outshone all the suns of all men's days.
Shall I not crown them with immortal praise
Whom I have loved, who have given me, dared with me
High secrets, and in darkness knelt to see
The inenarrable godhead of delight?

Love is a flame;—we have beaconed the world's night.
A city:—and we have built it, these and I.
An emperor:—we have taught the world to die.
So, for their sakes I loved, ere I go hence,
And the high cause of love's magnificence,
And to keep loyalties young, I'll write those names
Golden for ever, eagles, crying flames,
And set them as a banner, that man may know,
To dare the generations, burn, and blow
Out on the winds of time, shining and streaming . . .
These I have loved:
        White plates and cups, clean-gleaming,
Ringed with blue lines; and feathery, faery dust;
Wet roofs, beneath the lamp-light; the strong crust
Of friendly bread; and many-tasting food;
Rainbows; and the blue bitter smoke of wood;
And radiant raindrops couching in cool flowers;
And flowers themselves, that sway through sunny hours,
Dreaming of moths that drink them under the moon;
Then, the cool kindliness of sheets, that soon
Smooth away trouble; and the rough male kiss

Of blankets; grainy wood; live hair that is
Shining and free; blue-massing clouds; the keen
Unpassioned beauty of a great machine;
The benison of hot water; furs to touch;
The good smell of old clothes; and other such—
The comfortable smell of friendly fingers,
Hair's fragrance, and the musty reek that lingers
About dead leaves and last year's ferns . . .

                                  Dear names,
And thousand other throng to me! Royal flames;
Sweet water's dimpling laugh from tap or spring;
Holes in the ground; and voices that do sing;
Voices in laughter, too; and body's pain,
Soon turned to peace! and the deep-panting train;
Firm sands; the little dulling edge of foam
That browns and dwindles as the wave goes home;
And washen stones, gay for an hour; the cold
Graveness of iron; moist black earthen mould;
Sleep; and high places; footprints in the dew;
And oaks; and brown horse-chestnuts, glossy-new;
And new-peeled sticks; and shining pools on grass;—
All these have been my loves. And these shall pass,
Whatever passes not, in the great hour,
Nor all my passion, all my prayers, have power
To hold them with me through the gate of death.
They'll play deserter, turn with the traitor breath,
Break the high bond we made, and sell love's trust
And sacramented covenant to the dust.
—Oh, never a doubt but, somewhere, I shall wake,
And give what's left of love again, and make
New friends, now strangers . . . .
                        But the best I've known,

Stays here, and changes, breaks, grows old, is blown
About the winds of the world, and fades from brains
Of living men, and dies.

                            Nothing remains.
O dear my loves, O faithless, once again
This one last gift I give: that after men
Shall know, and later lovers, far-removed,
Praise you, "All these were lovely"; say, "He loved."

RUPERT BROOKE

MORNING SUN

Shuttles of trains going north, going south, drawing threads of
      blue,
The shining of the lines of trams like swords,
Thousands of posters asserting a monopoly of the good, the
      beautiful, the true,
Crowds of people all in the vocative, you and you,
The haze of the morning shot with words.

Yellow sun comes white off the wet streets but bright
Chromium yellows in the gay sun's light,
Filleted sun streaks the purple mist,
Everything is kissed and reticulated with sun
Scooped-up and cupped in the open fronts of shops
And bouncing on the traffic that never stops.

And the street fountain blown across the square
Rainbow-trellises the air and sunlight blazons
The red butcher's and scrolls of fish on marble slabs,

Whistled bars of music crossing silver sprays
And horns of cars, touché, touché, rapiers' retort, a moving
    cage,
A turning page of shine and sound, the day's maze.

But when the sun goes out, the streets go cold, the hanging
    meat
And tiers of fish are colourless and merely dead,
And the hoots of cars neurotically repeat and the tiptoed feet
Of women hurry and falter whose faces are dead;
And I see in the air but not belonging there
The blown grey powder of the fountain grey as the ash
That forming on a cigarette covers the red.

Louis MacNeice

THE DAY IS DONE

The day is done, and the darkness
    Falls from the wings of night,
As a feather is wafted downward
    From an eagle in his flight.

I see the lights of the village
    Gleam through the rain and the mist,
And a feeling of sadness comes o'er me,
    That my soul cannot resist:

A feeling of sadness and longing,
    That is not akin to pain,
And resembles sorrow only
    As the mist resembles the rain.

Come, read to me some poem,
   Some simple and heartfelt lay,
That shall soothe this restless feeling,
   And banish the thoughts of day.

Not from the grand old masters,
   Not from the bards sublime,
Whose distant footsteps echo
   Through the corridors of time.

For, like strains of martial music,
   Their mighty thoughts suggest
Life's endless toil and endeavour;
   And to night I long for rest.

Read from some humbler poet,
   Whose songs gushed from his heart,
As showers from the clouds of summer,
   Or tears from the eyelids start;

Who, through long days of labour,
   And nights devoid of ease,
Still heard in his soul the music
   Of wonderful melodies.

Such songs have power to quiet
   The restless pulse of care,
And come like the benediction
   That follows after prayer.

Then read from the treasured volume
   The poem of thy choice,
And lend to the rhyme of the poet
   The beauty of thy voice.

And the night shall be filled with music,
And the cares, that infest the day,
Shall fold their tents like the Arabs,
And as silently steal away.

HENRY WADSWORTH LONGFELLOW

GOD'S GRANDEUR

The world is charged with the grandeur of God.
It will flame out, like shining from shook foil;
It gathers to a greatness, like the ooze of oil
Crushed. Why do men then now not reck his rod?
Generations have trod, have trod, have trod;
And all is seared with trade; bleared, smeared with toil;
And wears man's smudge and shares man's smell: the soil
Is bare now, nor can foot feel, being shod.

And for all this, nature is never spent;
There lives the dearest freshness deep down things;
And though the last lights off the black west went
Oh, morning, at the brown brink eastward, springs—
Because the Holy Ghost over the bent
World broods with warm breast and with ah! bright wings.

GERARD MANLEY HOPKINS

CONQUISTADORS

Along the Rand in 'eighty-five
The veins of gold were torn,
Red houses rose among the rocks—
A plundering city was born.

Some who under the diamond stars
Had sailed the gilt-edged veld,
Wearing across their prow-like breasts
The order of the cartridge-belt,

Above their dream-entangled beards
Had steely, rock-drill eyes,
Cash-box conquistadors,
Anarchs of enterprise!

Some stole or cheated, some
Made off with their feverish gains,
And many failed, and a foolish few
Blew out their bankrupt brains.

Pioneers, O pioneers,
Grey pillars sunk in real estate,
How funny when the years have turned
Swashbuckler prim and scamp sedate!

Too late in memory's recesses
To find the nuggets of your prime,
Or recover the payable ore of youth
From the worked-out reef of time.

WILLIAM PLOMER

NIGHT CLOUDS

The white mares of the moon rush along the sky
Beating their golden hoofs upon the glass Heavens;
The white mares of the moon are all standing on their hind
    legs
Pawing at the green porcelain doors of the remote Heavens.
Fly, Mares!
Strain your utmost,
Scatter the milky dust of stars,
Or the tiger sun will leap upon you and destroy you
With one lick of his vermilion tongue.

AMY LOWELL

WHEN I SET OUT FOR LYONNESSE

When I set out for Lyonnesse,
  A hundred miles away,
  The rime was on the spray,
And starlight lit my lonesomeness
When I set out for Lyonnesse
  A hundred miles away.

What would bechance at Lyonnesse
  While I should sojourn there
  No prophet durst declare,
Nor did the wisest wizard guess
What would bechance at Lyonnesse
  While I should sojourn there.

When I came back from Lyonnesse
 With magic in my eyes,
 All marked with mute surmise
My radiance rare and fathomless,
When I came back from Lyonnesse
 With magic in my eyes!

THOMAS HARDY

THE ROAD NOT TAKEN

Two roads diverged in a yellow wood,
And sorry I could not travel both
And be one traveller, long I stood
And looked down one as far as I could
To where it bent in the undergrowth;

Then took the other, as just as fair,
And having perhaps the better claim,
Because it was grassy and wanted wear;
Though as for that the passing there
Had worn them really about the same,

And both that morning equally lay
In leaves no step had trodden black.
Oh, I kept the first for another day!
Yet knowing how way leads on to way,
I doubted if I should ever come back.

I shall be telling this with a sigh
Somewhere ages and ages hence:
Two roads diverged in a wood, and I—

I took the one less travelled by,
And that has made all the difference.

ROBERT FROST

ON FIRST LOOKING INTO
CHAPMAN'S HOMER

Much have I travell'd in the realms of gold
   And many goodly states and kingdoms seen;
   Round many western islands have I been
Which bards in fealty to Apollo hold.
Oft of one wide expanse had I been told
   That deep-brow'd Homer ruled as his demesne:
   Yet did I never breathe its pure serene
Till I heard Chapman speak out loud and bold:

Then felt I like some watcher of the skies
   When a new planet swims into his ken;
Or like stout Cortez, when with eagle eyes
   He stared at the Pacific—and all his men
Look'd at each other with a wild surmise—
   Silent, upon a peak in Darien.

JOHN KEATS

DEPARTURE IN THE DARK

Nothing so sharply reminds a man he is mortal
As leaving a place
In a winter morning's dark, the air on his face
Unkind as the touch of sweating metal:
Simple goodbyes to children or friends become
A felon's numb
Farewell, and love that was a warm, a meeting place—
Love is the suicide's grave under the nettles.

Gloomed and clemmed as if by an imminent ice-age
Lies the dear world
Of your street-strolling, field-faring. The senses, curled
At the dead end of a shrinking passage,
Care not if close the inveterate hunters creep,
And memories sleep
Like mammoths in lost caves. Drear, extinct is the world,
And has no voice for consolation or presage.

There is always something at such times of the passover,
When the dazed heart
Beats for it knows not what, whether you part
From home or prison, acquaintance or lover—
Something wrong with the time-table, something unreal
In the scrambled meal
And the bag ready packed by the door, as though the heart
Has gone ahead, or is staying here forever.

No doubt for the Israelites that early morning
It was hard to be sure
If home were prison or prison home: the desire
Going forth meets the desire returning.

This land, that had cut their pride down to the bone
Was now their own
By ancient deeds of sorrow. Beyond, there was nothing sure
But a desert of freedom to quench their fugitive yearnings.

At this blind hour the heart is informed of nature's
Ruling that man
Should be nowhere a more tenacious settler than
Among wry thorns and ruins, yet nurture
A seed of discontent in his ripest ease.
There's a kind of release
And a kind of torment in every goodbye for every man—
And will be, even to the last of his dark departures.

C. Day Lewis

Biographies and Notes

ANONYMOUS POETS

TRUE THOMAS (page 61)

Thomas — Thomas the Rymer of Erceldoune, who was supposed to have lived in the thirteenth century. As well as delivering prophecies, he was also the reputed author of "Sir Tristrem," the earliest specimen of Scottish poetry. True Thomas' story echoes the tale of Tannhäuser, in which a mortal singer is seduced by an immortal queen. The story of True Thomas was rewritten by John Keats three hundred years later as a modern ballad, which he called "La Belle Dame Sans Merci." This poem may be found on page 64.

STANZA ONE: **The Eildon Tree** — under this tree of magic Thomas delivered his prophecies. STANZA FIVE: **Harp and carp** — play and talk lightly. STANZA SIX: **Betide me weal, betide me woe** — whether good or bad fortune befalls me. STANZA TEN: **light down** — get down. STANZA TWELVE: **lily leven** — lovely lawn. STANZA SIXTEEN: **mirk** — dark, misty, dense. STANZA EIGHTEEN: **tryst** — meeting place. STANZA TWENTY: **even cloth** — smooth cloth.

ANDERSON, PATRICK (1915 —)

Born in England and educated at Oxford University and Columbia in New York, where he held a Commonwealth Foundation, he became a member of the English Department at McGill University in Montreal. In 1950 he accepted a lectureship in English at the University of Malaya in Singapore, and in 1953 he returned to London to teach at the University of London.

SLEIGHRIDE (page 42)

STANZA ONE: **gauche** — without ease or grace. STANZA FOUR:
like shuttle in slot — like a bobbin in a groove. **roughhouse** —
disturbance or row; horseplay. **retching** — making the sound of
vomiting. **an Adam in Time** — The newness or uniqueness of the
experience is like the beginning of man's life. **the two in blue with
velvet heads** — the shadows in the snow of the two passengers.
STANZA SEVEN: **lane** — the narrow street on which the sleigh is
riding. **alteration** — a change in position or situation, since the
experience is a new one for him. **the terror of Time** — The feeling
that he is somehow back at the beginning of time is a frightening
one.

AUDEN, WYSTAN HUGH (1907 —)

Born in York, England, he was educated at Gresham's School
and Christ College, Oxford. He became the leader of a group of
poets that included Stephen Spender and C. D. Lewis, whose works
were left-wing, and who were all greatly influenced by T. S. Eliot.
In 1939 he took up residence in America, where he lectured at
various colleges and universities. In 1956 he was appointed Professor of Poetry at Oxford.

THE UNKNOWN CITIZEN (page 113)

the Greater Community — the state. **scab** — a worker who con-
tinues to work when the union is on strike. **our report . . . Our
social psychology workers** — the state's. **Eugenist** — authority on
the production of fine human offspring.

AVISON, MARGARET KIRKLAND (1918 —)

Born in Galt, Ontario, she received her higher education at
University of Toronto. In 1956 she was awarded the Guggenheim
Fellowship in Poetry. A resident of Toronto, Ontario, she writes
poetry that has been termed metaphysical, in the manner that the
late Wallace Stevens' poetry is metaphysical. A book of her poetry,
Winter Sun, was published in 1960, and a second, *The Dumbfound-
ing*, in 1967.

SNOW (page 42)

optic heart — the heart in search of visual experience. **sedges** — grasslike plants growing in marshes or by the water-side. **pewter** — grey alloy of tin and lead. **rhizomes** — horizontal stems emitting roots. **trundle** — roll. **candy-bright disks** — the snowflakes. **legend** — inscription, meaning. **colour of mourning** — White is the colour of mourning in China; thus, the white of the snowflakes is associated with death. **Yangtze** — river in China whose floods have killed thousands; also a source of life since its valley is one of the most fertile. **stasis** — standstill; arrest. **this starry blur** — this one particular snowflake. **the rest** — the rest of the snowflakes. **may ring your change** — Literally, the expression "ring the changes" refers to the different orders in which the peal of bells may be rung; figuratively, the expression means to exhaust the ways of putting or doing a thing. Therefore, all the snowflakes, taken together, may exhaust all the possibilities for thought or expression, since each snowflake is unique and there are millions of them.

THAW (page 44)

STANZA ONE: **roots of sky** — the bottom, the source or origin of the sky. **moodier sky** — the sky as it appears reflected in the muddy ice-water. STANZA THREE: **lime-water** — grey, cloudy water mixed with the earth. **the dogless pale pale blue** — Either there are no stars in the sky (i.e. no constellations of the Greater or Lesser Dogs, and no Sirius, the dog star), or these are hardly "dog days" or hot days of the year. STANZA FIVE: **the Black Death**—During the Great Plague in the fourteenth century people engaged in strange superstitious practices, including dancing, in order to ward off death. **the silt of centuries** — the layers of earth that have buried civilizations of the past.

BENÉT, STEPHEN VINCENT (1898-1943)

Born in Bethlehem, Pennsylvania, he spent his boyhood in California and Georgia, where his father was stationed at various army camps. He entered Yale at seventeen and in the same year published his first volume, entitled *Five Men and Pompey*. In 1928, Benét published *John Brown's Body*, for which he received a Pulitzer prize.

JACK ELLYAT (page 71)

Stanza One: **Jack Ellyat** — a volunteer from Connecticut in the Northern army, fighting in the first Battle of Bull Run, July 21, 1861. At Bull Run, a stream in Virginia, the Northern forces were completely routed. **a red sop** — a wet bloodstain. **rebels** — southern Confederate soldiers.

BIRNEY, ALFRED EARLE (1904 —)

Born in Calgary, Alberta, he was educated at the Universities of British Columbia, Toronto, California, and London. His reputation as a poet was established by his *David And Other Poems,* published in 1942. Before World War II, he was Assistant Professor of English at University College, University of Toronto, and after returning from overseas, he was appointed Professor of English, University of British Columbia. Mr. Birney is now poet-in-residence at University of Toronto.

CAN. LIT. (page 6)

Can. Lit. — an abbreviation for Canadian Literature. **eagles** — people with great literary talent. **aeromantic** — derived from a combination of *aero*, meaning "airy", and *romantic*, meaning "remote from experience, impractical." **ties** — railway ties. **Emily** —Emily Dickinson, an American poet, who since her death has become known for her penetrating poetic statement. **Whitman** — Walt Whitman, a famous American poet, whose thought and writing were products of the American Civil War. (Poems written by both Whitman and Dickinson are included in this anthology.)

DAVID (page 32)

I — **ruck** — heap. **fetid** — smelly. II — **faceted** — like the small, polished surfaces of a cut diamond. **skree** — broken rock. **larches** — coniferous trees. **gentian** — plant with blue and yellow flowers. **saxifrage** — rock plant. III — **arête** — the sharp ascending ridge of a mountain. **hawks** — The original word used here was *kites*, but the poet has recently changed the word to refer to birds more indigenous to the Canadian Rockies. IV — **pika** — small rodents resembling rabbits. **trilobites** — fossils. **Cambrian** — one of the early geological periods. V — **col** — depression in a mountain chain. **scarp** — steep slope. **lobbed** — tossed. **gyrating** — moving in circles. VII — **bighorns** — Rocky Mountain sheep. **moraine** — a heap of earth and rocks deposited by a glacier. **séracs** — large, angular blocks of glacial ice. **chimney** — narrow vertical cleft in a rock-face. VIII — **cirque** — a circular recess formed by deep cliffs. IX — **bergschrund** — a crevasse or gap at the head of a glacier. **névé** — an expanse of granular snow not yet compressed into ice at the head of a glacier. **slug** — a shell-less snail that is destructive to small plants.

BLAKE, WILLIAM (1757-1827)

Born in London, he was the son of a well-to-do hosier. He had no formal education, and at the age of fourteen he was apprenticed to an engraver. His engravings are now as famous as his poetry. His two best-known books of poetry are *Songs of Innocence* and *Songs of Experience.*

THE TYGER (page 127)

STANZA ONE: **symmetry** — balanced form. STANZA TWO: **deeps** — deep parts of the sea; also pits or abysses. **he** — the creator of the tiger, a reference to the "immortal hand or eye" in stanza one. **aspire** — soar. **seize the fire** — The creator here appears to be a blacksmith. STANZA THREE: **the sinews of thy heart** — The phrase emphasizes the strength and hardness of the tiger's heart. **dread hand, dread feet** — The awe felt by the poet for the creator of the tiger is increasing. STANZA FOUR: **Dare its deadly terrors clasp** — Here the poet's feeling of awe is replaced by fear and even terror. STANZA FIVE: **When the stars threw down their spears** — possibly a reference to the shedding of light rays. **the Lamb** — a traditional symbol of goodness, innocence, and love; Christ.

BROOKE, RUPERT (1887-1915)

Born at Rugby, the son of a schoolmaster, he was educated at the famous boys' school of Rugby and at Cambridge where he became a tutor. At the beginning of the First World War he joined the navy and in 1915 sailed for the assault on the Dardanelles, but before reaching there he died of blood-poisoning. He was a poet of great promise, whose death had the immediate effect of stemming much of the romantic idealism generated by World War I.

THE GREAT LOVER (page 168)

STANZA ONE: **my night** — my death. **a star** — a sign of love; hence, his poem. **them** — In the second stanza he lists the things he loves. **inenarrable** — indescribable. STANZA TWO: faery dust — with supernatural qualities. **benison** — jug. STANZA THREE: **And these shall pass** — All is transitory. **in the great hour** — in death. **They'll play deserter** — They will desert me when I die. **somewhere I shall wake** — He believes in his own immortality. STANZA FOUR: **last line** — The things he has left behind will be loved by others both for their own worth and for their association with the poet.

BROWNING, ELIZABETH BARRETT (1806-1861)

Born near Durham, England, she read Homer in Greek at age eight. At twelve she wrote *The Battle of Marathon,* an "epic" of four books. At fifteen a horse fall caused a spinal injury which compelled her to live as an invalid. When she was already famous as a poet, she met and married the then little-known Robert Browning. Because of her ill health, they spent most of their lives in Italy, where she died. Her most famous work is *Sonnets From The Portuguese.*

HOW DO I LOVE THEE (page 57)

This is one of a number of sonnets written in 1845 and published after her marriage as a collection, entitled *Sonnets From The Portuguese.* Browning's pet name for his wife was "my little Portuguese," which referred to her sallow complexion induced by long illness.

the ends of being — the purposes of existence. **ideal grace** — the unmerited favour of God; a divine regenerating and inspiring influence. **I shall but love thee better after death** — She did not expect to live long when she wrote this sonnet.

BROWNING, ROBERT (1812-1889)

Born at Camberwell in London and privately educated, he decided to be a poet at age fourteen. His first poem, "Pauline" was published in 1833. He developed the dramatic monologue as a poetic form, and his verse reflected his own vigorous and optimistic personality. After the death of his wife, Elizabeth Barrett, he moved from Italy to London where he became socially prominent, being recognized as the greatest living poet after Tennyson.

MY LAST DUCHESS (page 148)

SECTION ONE: **Fra Pandolf** — a character invented by the poet, who is a member of a religious brotherhood. **that pictured countenance** — the face in the painting. SECTION TWO: **my favour** — some piece of jewellery. **some officious fool** — some person trying to curry her favour by doing more than is appropriate. **set her wits to yours** — argued. SECTION THREE: **known munificence** — "munificence" is more flattering than "generosity." **is ample warrant that . . . be disallowed** — is guarantee that any reasonable request by me for dowry will be acceptable.

BURNS, ROBERT (1759-1796)

Best loved of all Scottish poets, Burns was born of humble parents at Alloway near Ayr. His best poetry was written in the native Scottish dialect. In 1786 he published *Poems Chiefly in Scottish Dialect*, which made him instantly famous.
JOHN ANDERSON, MY JO (page 58)

STANZA ONE: **jo** — love, sweetheart. **brent** — smooth, unwrinkled. **pow** — head. STANZA TWO: **cantie** — happy. **maun** — must.

COLERIDGE, SAMUEL TAYLOR (1772-1834)

Born at Ottery Saint Mary, Devonshire, England, he was educated at Blue-Coat School and at Cambridge. In collaboration with William Wordsworth he published *Lyrical Ballads* in 1798. He was able to produce poetry until 1800 when he fell victim to the opium habit. One of his most famous poems is "The Rime Of The Ancient Mariner."

KUBLA KHAN (page 134)

STANZA ONE: **In Xanadu did Kubla Khan** — Coleridge was reading about Kubla Khan in *Purchas His Pilgrim*, an Elizabethan travel book, when he fell asleep; during his sleep he composed the poem. **Xanadu** — a region in China. **Kubla Khan** — founder of the Mongol dynasty in China. **sinuous rills** — winding streams. **measure** — music. STANZA TWO: **dulcimer** — the prototype of a piano; a musical instrument with strings of graduated length over a sounding board or box that is struck with hammers. **Abora** — possibly Abba Gared, a mountain in Ethiopia said to have been an earthly paradise. **I would build that dome in air** — I would remake the pleasure-dome in another art form, that of poetry. **And all should cry, Beware!** Everyone would then be frightened of my magical poetic powers. **weave a circle** — cast a spell. **honey-dew, milk of Paradise** — supernatural foods.

COLOMBO, JOHN (1936 —)

Born in Kitchener, Ontario, he is a graduate of the University of Toronto. He is presently an editor-at-large in Toronto and managing editor of *The Tamarack Review*, Canada's leading literary quarterly. His publications include *The Mackenzie Poems*, a collection of the writings of William Lyon Mackenzie, arranged in such a way as to reveal the poetic qualities of his prose; *The Great Wall of China*; and *Abracadabra*, 1967.

IMMIGRANTS (page 11)

The source for this "found" poem by Mr. Colombo is Margaret Fairley's collection of papers, letters, and speeches, entitled *The Selected Writings of William Lyon Mackenzie*. Mackenzie, who was born in 1795 near Dundee, Scotland, emigrated to York, the capital of Upper Canada, where he became involved in politics both as a representative in the House of Assembly and as the founder of the newspaper, *The Colonial Advocate*. For his activities against the Family Compact, the establishment that ruled the colony, his printing press was smashed and his type thrown into Lake Ontario. In 1837 Mackenzie led an unsuccessful rebellion in Toronto, and briefly established headquarters for a provisional government on Navy Island near Niagara Falls. He left Canada to work on the *New York Tribune*, but returned thirteen years later to continue his newspaper work in Canada. He died in 1861.

CUMMINGS, EDWARD ESTLIN (1894-1962)

Born in Cambridge, Massachussetts, where his father taught English at Harvard, Cummings was educated at Harvard, and later served in the Ambulance Corps during World War I. When he was about thirty years old, he published his first volume of poems, *Tulips and Chimneys*, a book that was considered original to the point of eccentricity. His poems are noted for their lack of traditional form; lines of verse are broken, and a minimum of punctuation is used.

SPRING IS LIKE A PERHAPS HAND (page 95)

STANZA ONE: **a perhaps hand** — a hand associated with speculation and probability, as opposed to fact; the hand of God or of nature. **Nowhere** — The word is capitalized because it names a place. **arranging a window** — the unseen hand is like that of a window-dresser.

NEXT TO OF COURSE GOD (page 152)

Land of the pilgrims — part of an American song. **say can you see by the dawn's early** — part of the first line of the American national anthem. **my country 'tis of** — a snatch of another American patriotic song. **by gorry . . . by gum** — American slang.

DE LA MARE, WALTER (1873-1956)

Born in Kent, England, of Huguenot descent, he was related through his mother to Robert Browning. He was educated at St. Paul's Cathedral school, later spending eighteen years of his life employed by an oil company. The publication of *The Listeners and Other Poems* in 1912 established his reputation.

SUNK LYONESSE (page 121)

Lyonesse — the mythical underwater homeland of King Arthur. (See also "When I Set Out For Lyonesse" by Thomas Hardy, p. 176) **Nereids** — sea-nymphs. **casemate** — a vaulted chamber in the wall of one of the fortresses or castles. **With fire in his skull for torch** — a reference to a species of fish which has its own incandescence. **ringing wires** — the strings of the lyres. **the sullen courts of sleep** — Everything is dead in Lyonesse. **for aye** — forever. **His stone-ribbed side** — The carver of the flowers is likewise dead.

DICKINSON, EMILY (1830-1886)

Born in Amherst, Massachussetts, where she lived most of her life, she entered South Hadley Female Seminary, disliked it immediately, and returned home a confirmed rebel. At twenty-three she spent a few weeks in Washington with her father, whom she adored, and a short time in Philadelphia. After her return to Amherst, she became a recluse. She rarely crossed the threshold; even in her house, visitors saw her only as a figure vanishing down a corridor. Her fame rests on the innumerable poems found after her death.

I FELT A FUNERAL IN MY BRAIN (page 70)

STANZA ONE: **I felt a funeral** — I imagined what it was like to die, and to attend my own funeral. **that sense was breaking through** — The experience was meaningful in that it showed her what death is like. STANZA THREE: **a box** — her coffin. **boots of lead** — heavy, noisy boots. STANZA FOUR: **a bell** — her death knell. **Being** — life, existence. **I and silence some strange race** — Because of the ringing of the heavens, she, the listener, like silence, is out of place.

THE GRASS (page 90)

STANZA FOUR: **spikenards** — aeromatic ointments or fragrant oils.

THE SNAKE (page 100)

STANZA TWO: **shaft** — slender stick; ray of lightning; a long-bow arrow. STANZA THREE: **whiplash** — the quick motion of a tightly twisted cord used for punishing. **unbraiding** — unwinding of the snake's coils. STANZA FOUR: **transport** — vehement emotion.

THE RAILROAD TRAIN (page 122)

STANZA ONE: **prodigious** — marvellous; enormous. STANZA TWO: **supercilious** — haughty, contemptuous. **a quarry pare** — cut an excavation through the mountains. STANZA FOUR: **Boanerges** — a loud-voiced preacher or orator; derived from a Hebrew word meaning sons of thunder.

DONNE, JOHN (1573-1631)

Born in London, he was educated at Oxford and Cambridge. He accompanied the Earl of Essex as a volunteer in his expeditions to Cadiz in 1596 and the Azores in 1597. In 1614 he was ordained in the Anglican Church and later became Dean of St. Paul's, a position which he filled with great distinction until his death. As well as being a famous poet, he was regarded as one of the greatest preachers of his day.

SONG (page 60)

STANZA ONE: **mandrake root** — the root of a poisonous plant, which is supposed to represent human form and to shriek when plucked. **the Devil's foot** — like the cleft hoof of the god, Pan.

A HYMN TO GOD THE FATHER (page 168)

I — **that sin where I begun** — original sin. **those sins, through which I run** — the sins I continue to commit. **thou hast not done** — a pun on his own name; God has not finished forgiving Donne, for there are more sins yet to be confessed; also God does not have Donne in a state ready to receive divine grace. II — **that sin by which I have won/Others** — his sin of causing others to sin. **my sin their door** — His sin, like a door, opened or gave access to sins by others. III — **My last thread** — when my life is at an end. **I shall perish on the shore** — My soul shall *not* become immortal. **thy son/Shall shine . . .** — Christ shall be with me as he is now and was before. **Thou hast done** — God's task of forgiving Donne is now finished; also He now has Donne in a state to receive divine grace.

ECCLESIASTES 12: 1-19

REMEMBER NOW THY CREATOR (page 76)

while the sun . . . darkened — While you still have sight. **the house** — the physical body. **the grinders** — the teeth. **the windows** — the eyes. **the doors** — possibly the lips. **shall be brought low** — cannot be heard because of deafness. **the almond tree shall flourish** — the hair will turn white like the almond blossom. **the silver cord** — the thread of life. **the golden bowl** — This was believed to hold a person's spirit during life.

ELIOT, THOMAS STEARNS (1888-1965)

Born in St. Louis, Missouri, of a distinguished Boston family, he was educated at Harvard, the Sorbonne in Paris, and Oxford. Mr. Eliot has been referred to as "in all probability the greatest poetic influence of our time." In 1915 he took up residence in England and became a naturalized British subject in 1927. After teaching at Highgate, he joined the foreign department of Lloyds Bank. In 1922 he founded *The Criterion*, the best English literary review of its time, and soon after became a director of the publishing house of Faber and Faber, a post which he held until his death. The Order of Merit was bestowed on Mr. Eliot in 1948, and his enormous influence on contemporary writing was also recognized by the award of the Nobel Prize for Literature.

THE HOLLOW MEN (page 106)

I — **The Old Guy** — The execution of Guy Fawkes for his part in the Gunpowder Plot of 1605 is still celebrated in England on November 5, when children set off fireworks and burn effigies of "The Old Guy", begging pennies in return. "The Old Guy" in the poem, like the scarecrow, is another symbol of the hollow men. **with direct eyes** — Those who have experienced spiritual regeneration. **death's other kingdom** — heaven; perhaps real death, as opposed to living death. II — **Eyes I dare not meet** — The hollow man who is speaking is spiritually blind; he cannot look directly at people or life. **death's dream kingdom** — living death on earth. **sunlight on a broken column** — what is seen by the spiritually blind; a symbol of man's failure. **Let me be no nearer** — I am content that the situation remain as it is; I do not want to experience spiritual regeneration. **Rat's coat, crowskin, crossed staves** — the frock coat, tall black hat, and wooden frame of a scarecrow. **Not that final meeting** — I shrink from that last meeting with eternal truth somewhere between this world and the next. III — **the dead land** — the spiritual wasteland. **the stone images** — symbols of false and meaningless worship. IV — **this hollow valley** — the Valley of the Shadow of Death. **the tumid river** — the swollen and foul river Styx which divides the world of the living from the world of the dead. **multifoliate rose** — the many-petalled rose which represents eternity; in association with the star, the only sign of hope. V — **Here we go round the prickly pear** — a parody of the children's game, "Here we go round the mulberry bush." **prickly pear** — species of cactus. **Shadow** — the fear that there is no existence beyond death. **This is the way the world ends** — a parody of the children's song.

THE JOURNEY OF THE MAGI (page 129)

See also "The Magi" by W. B. Yeats, page 129.

STANZA ONE: **first five lines** — adapted from part of a Christmas sermon by Bishop Lancelot Andrewes (1555-1626). **galled** — covered with saddle sores. **refractory** — bad-tempered and difficult to manage. **voices** — the voices of those who had tried to dissuade them. **three trees** — symbolic of the three crosses at Calvary. **white horse** — See Revelations 6:2 and 19: 11. **lintel** — horizontal timber or stone over door or window. **dicing** — foreshadowing of the Roman soldiers dicing beside the Cross. **pieces of silver** — foreshadowing of the betrayal of Jesus by Judas Iscariot. STANZA TWO: **our death** — the death of our old ways, our old beliefs. **alien people** — They are now alien because they have not undergone the same change in spiritual values and beliefs as the Wise Men. **another death** — physical death.

FERLINGHETTI, LAWRENCE (1919 —)

Born in Yonkers, New York, the son of an auctioneer, Ferlinghetti attended the University of North Carolina, Columbia, and the Sorbonne. After World War II he worked for *Time* magazine. He founded the first all-paperbound bookstore in the United States, called City Lights, in San Francisco and is principal owner and editor-in-chief of City Lights Books and the Pocket Poet series. His books of poetry include *A Coney Island of the Mind* and *Starting From San Francisco*, published in 1958 and 1961 respectively.

JUST AS I USED TO SAY (page 159)

the sly switch — the switch that sends them unexpectedly onto a different track. **caboose** — the last car of the train, used by the trainmen for eating and relaxing. **new electric horns** — no longer the same as the old whistles of steam trains. **rusty spur** — an unused track off to the side of the main track. **the bright saloon** — the caboose.

FINCH, ROBERT (1900 —)

Born in Freeport, Long Island, New York, he began writing poetry as an undergraduate at University of Toronto. After post-graduate work in Paris, he returned to Toronto as a Professor of French. His first book, *Poems,* published in 1946, won the Governor-General's Award. His latest book is *Silverthorn Bush and Other Poems.*

THE STATUE (page 46)

STANZA ONE: **rustle** — From a distance, in contrast to the stillness of the statue, the three people appear to be moving like leaves. STANZA TWO: **cudgels** — The upthrust of the fountains is like the brandishing of weapons. **blue netting** — The sky appears to have captured the boy in its netting. STANZA THREE: **stone axis** — The statue resembles a straight line about which the three are rotating.

TRAIN WINDOW (page 124)

STANZA ONE: **a paradigm** — an example or pattern, especially of the inflection of a noun, verb, or other part of speech. STANZA TWO: **a transitory Icehenge** — The cakes of melting ice remind the poet of the rocks at Stonehenge, an ancient place of Druid worship in England. **imitation snow** — ice chips. STANZA THREE: **stiffened frosted caracul** — The mottled effect of the galvanized pails resembles old Astrakhan fur coats made stiff with the snows of winter. **frozen elocution, running chalk-talk** — The phrases indicate the communication between the pails and the boxcars.

FLECKER, JAMES ELROY (1884-1915)

Born at Lewisham, England, he was educated at Oxford and Cambridge where he studied Oriental languages. He was posted to the consular service at Constantinople and later at Beirut. He died of consumption in Davos, Switzerland.

TO A POET A THOUSAND YEARS HENCE (page 132)

STANZA TWO: **consummate** — complete, perfect. STANZA FOUR: **Maeonides** — a name sometimes applied to Homer.

FROST, ROBERT (1875-1963)

Born in San Francisco, he lived with his mother at the Frost homestead in Lawrence, Massachussetts, after his father died. At seventeen he entered Dartmouth College, but remained there only several months. He married at twenty, went to Harvard, and left after two years without a degree. During the next few years Frost was a mill worker, a school teacher, a farmer, and a poet. Unable to achieve recognition in the United States, he took his family to England, and in 1913 published his first book of poems, *A Boy's Will*, which was followed by *North of Boston* in 1914. In 1915 he returned to America. He was now in his fortieth year, unknown and without money. With the American publication of *North of Boston*, however, Frost became famous. Critics praised his stern bucolics which were so different from the traditional English pastorals. While sometimes severe, his poetry shows a mature philosophy and sympathetic mind.

GRAVES, ROBERT (1895 —)

Born in London, England, he was educated at Charterhouse and St. John's College, Oxford. During the first World War he served with the Royal Welsh Fusilliers in France and it was officially reported that he had "died of wounds" on his twenty-first birthday. He survived to read English at Oxford, and for one year became

Professor of English Literature at Cairo, on the recommendation of T. E. Lawrence. During the thirties he worked in Majorca, Spain, where he ran the Seizin Press, publishing a number of books and critical articles. He came back to England during the Spanish Civil War, and lived there until 1947, when he returned to Majorca. In 1961 he was elected Professor of Poetry at Oxford in succession to W. H. Auden.

IN THE WILDERNESS (page 128)

the lost desert-folk — the creatures of the wilderness, all of whom are lonely outcasts. **the bittern's call** — the booming note of the marsh bird. **the she-pelican** — See Psalm 111:6 — "I am like the pelican of the wilderness." **Basilisk, cockatrice** — fabulous serpents hatched from cock's eggs, said to be so poisonous that even their glance is fatal; representatives of all monstrous and distorted things. **homilies** — sermons. **mail** — armour. **great rats on leather wings** — bats. **scape-goat** — Traditionally, the goat was allowed to escape into the wilderness when the Jewish chief priest had symbolically laid the sins of his people on it. See Leviticus 16.

GRAY, THOMAS (1716-1771)

Born in London and educated at Eton and Cambridge, Gray was one of the most learned scholars of his period. He travelled in Europe with Horace Walpole, quarrelled with him, and returned to the village of Stoke Poges. It was there, after his reconciliation with Walpole, that he sent his friend "An Elegy Written In A Country Churchyard."

ELEGY WRITTEN IN A COUNTRY CHURCHYARD (page 154)

STANZA TWO: **tinklings** — the sound of sheep bells. **bow'r** — dwelling. STANZA THREE: **yew-tree** — traditionally associated with death. **rude** — simple, uneducated. STANZA SEVEN: **sickle** — reaping hook. **glebe** — earth. **jocund** — merry, sprightly. STANZA EIGHT: **annals** — history, life story. STANZA TEN: **aisle** — long passage down the centre of a church. **fretted vault** — ornamented stone ceiling. STANZA ELEVEN: **storied urn** — monument with inscription. STANZA TWELVE: **rod of empire** — governing power. **living lyre** — poetry. STANZA THIRTEEN: **penury** — poverty. STANZA FIFTEEN: **village Hampden** — John Hampden, an English commoner who dared to oppose Charles I, and in so doing awoke his countrymen to the need for the curtailment of royal power. STANZA EIGHTEEN: **the blushes of ingenuous shame** — their own natural modesty. STANZA NINETEEN: **cool sequester'd vale**—the quiet secluded valley. **tenor** — even course. STANZA TWENTY-ONE: **rustic moralist** — the countryman who draws a moral from tombstones. STANZA TWENTY-TWO: **to dumb forgetfulness a prey** — destined soon to be forgotten. **pleasing anxious being** — an existence that brings both happiness and sadness. STANZA TWENTY-THREE: **cries** — protests against oblivion. **wonted** — accustomed. STANZA TWENTY-FOUR: **For thee** — as for thee. STANZA TWENTY-NINE: **the lay** — the lines or verses on his tombstone. **thorn** — hawthorn tree. STANZA THIRTY: **science** — knowledge. **frown'd not** — looked favourably. STANZA THIRTY-ONE: **recompense** — reward. STANZA THIRTY-TWO: **frailties** — weaknesses.

GUNN, THOM (1929 —)

Born at Gravesend, England, he was educated at University College School, London, and at Cambridge. His first volume of poetry, *Fighting Terms*, was published in 1954. He has lived in Rome, and has continued his education as teacher and student at Stanford and the University of California at Berkeley. Mr. Gunn is one of England's brightest young poets.

BLACK JACKETS (page 118)

STANZA ONE: **rawly** — in a manner that crudely exposes. STANZA TWO: **leather** — the leather of his jacket. STANZA THREE: **remote exertion** — efforts made a long time ago. **insignia** — marks or creases worn in the leather. STANZA FOUR: **concocting selves for their impervious kit** — manufacturing images or outward appearances for themselves that are incapable of being harmed or damaged. STANZA FIVE: **the Bay** — San Francisco Bay. STANZA SEVEN: **loss** — failure, represented by his motorcycle jacket. **complicity** — partnership in an action outside the law or accepted code of behaviour.

HARDY, THOMAS (1840-1928)

Born in Dorsetshire, England, he used the Wessex landscape as background for much of his work. His father was a stonemason, and as a boy Hardy was apprenticed to an architect. At twenty-three he won a prize offered by the Royal Institute of British Architects, and studied at King's College, London. Poetry, however, commanded his devotion; but finding little recognition, he turned to writing novels. He wrote his first novel, *Desperate Remedies*, at the age of thirty. During the next twenty-five years he published a dozen widely acclaimed novels. In 1895, upon the publication of *Jude The Obscure*, he was attacked as "immoral," and was so deeply offended that, as he said, "it cured me of all interest in novel writing." Hardy was acknowledged to be the greatest English poet of his day.

WHEN I SET OUT FOR LYONESSE (page 176)

See notes on "Sunk Lyonesse," by Walter de la Mare, page 121.

STANZA ONE: **Lyonesse** — a mythical, far-off land said to be submerged under water, the birthplace of King Arthur. **rime** — hoarfrost. **spray** — spray of bushes; or the spray of the ocean. STANZA TWO: **bechance** — happen. **sojourn** — stay. **durst** — dare. STANZA THREE: **mute surmise** — silent wonder.

HOPKINS, GERARD MANLEY (1844-1889)

Born at Stratford, Essex, he was educated at Balliol College, Oxford. At age twenty-three, Hopkins became a Roman Catholic and burned his early verses. Eleven years later, he was ordained to the priesthood as a Jesuit. After serving as a missionary in Liverpool, he was given a church in Oxford. At forty he was appointed to the chair of Greek at University College, Dublin. He continued his work in the Dublin slums, and it was there that he contracted typhoid fever, which was the cause of his death at forty-five. His poetry was not published until thirty years after his death, at which time Robert Bridges, his literary executor, felt that literary fashion had changed sufficiently for an appreciation of Hopkin's work.

THE CAGED SKYLARK (page 95)

dare-gale — carefree and courageous in braving the fiercest gales. **scanted** — barely existed. **bone-house** — body, as opposed to spirit. **his free fells** — his sky-diving. **spells** — charms, incantations. **their barriers** — that which confines them; namely, the cage of the bird and the earthly, bodily life of man. **uncumbered** — unhampered.

GOD'S GRANDEUR (page 174)

STANZA ONE: **charged** — electrically charged. **shook foil** — silver foil, which, when shaken, gives off static electricity. **gathers to a greatness** — coheres. **reck** — know, appreciate. **his rod** — God's power. STANZA TWO: **spent** — worn out, finished. **broods** — like a protective mother hen.

HOUSMAN, ALFRED EDWARD (1859-1936)

Housman was born in Shropshire, the county which became the scene of his poetry. His father was a lawyer. Young Housman was educated at St. John's College, Oxford, where he failed an important examination which shattered his hopes of an immediate scholastic appointment at a large university. Consequently, he was forced to work as a clerk in the Patent Office. During the ten years of his clerkship, he spent every spare hour in the study of the classics, and in 1892 was made professor of Latin at University College, London. He remained at University College for twenty years, and in 1911 went to Cambridge University, where he taught and lectured almost until the day of his death.

WHEN I WAS ONE-AND-TWENTY (page 59)

STANZA ONE: **fancy** — individual taste or inclination (fancy free — not in love). STANZA TWO: **rue** — repentance, dejection.

HUGHES, LANGSTON (1902 —)

Born in Joplin, Missouri, a Negro, he was brought up by his grandmother. His first poems were published in the magazine of Cleveland Central High School, which he attended. After spending a year at Columbia University, he worked as a trans-Atlantic seaman, a Paris cook, and a bus-boy at Wardman Park Hotel in New York, where Vachel Lindsay took an interest in his poetry. The publication of *The Weary Blues* in 1925 led to a scholarship, and to the completion of his education at Lincoln University in Pennsylvania. Since that time he has written novels, short stories, plays, motion picture scripts, and further poetry.

THE WEARY BLUES (page 166)

syncopated — the beats or accents in a musical passage are displaced so that what was strong becomes weak, and vice versa. **Lenox Avenue** — the main street in Harlem, New York. **raggy** — syncopated.

HUGHES, TED (1930 —)

Born in the Pennine area of the West Riding of Yorkshire, England, he was educated at Wexborough Grammar School and Pembroke College, Cambridge University. After graduation in 1954, he worked as a gardener, night-watchman, and script reader at Pinewood Film Studios. Since 1956 he has devoted himself to writing and teaching.

AN OTTER (page 101)

STANZA ONE: **an eel's/ oil of water body** — covered with the same kind of slippery oil that is found on the body of an eel. **four-legged yet water-gifted** — The otter is an aquatic fish-eating mammal. STANZA TWO: **the legend of himself** — his past history and his present existence. **before wars or burials** — He was on the earth before man was. **hounds and vermin-poles** — He has survived despite enemies such as hounds and weasel-like creatures. **Does not take root like the badger** — does not burrow in the ground like the badger, an animal which otherwise closely resembles the otter. **melting** — the quick and quiet motion of the otter as it enters the water almost invisibly. STANZA THREE: **some world lost** — an earlier, prehistoric world. **cleaves the stream's push** — cuts into the current and swims against it. STANZA FOUR: **like a king in hiding** — as if he were a deposed ruler or pretender to a kingdom unknown to man. **the bats** — lonely creatures that travel blindly across the earth; a parallel to the otter. **walloping** — moving awkwardly and noisily.

JOHNSON, EMILY PAULINE (1862-1913)

Born on the Six Nations Reserve south of Brantford, Ontario, Miss Johnson was the daughter of the Mohawk chief, George Henry Martin Johnson, and Emily Howells of a white missionary family. Although she did not go beyond primary school, she had read Scott and Longfellow before age thirteen, and at that age was studying Byron and Shakespeare. Her first book of verse, *The White Wampum*, published in 1894, along with her public poetry recitals, made her the darling of both Canada and England. Her complete works can be found in *Flint and Feather*.

THE LEGEND OF QU'APPELLE VALLEY (page 21)

Qu'Appelle — the French word for "who calls." (The Cree word, incidentally, is *Katepwa*.) The Qu'Appelle Valley is located approximately sixty-five miles north-east of Regina, Saskatchewan. It is a long, narrow cut in the prairie, made by glaciers. A chain of lakes runs through the valley. Two of them, Lake Katepwa and Echo Lake, along with the nearby town of Fort Qu'Appelle, are named for the legend.

KEATS, JOHN (1795-1821)

Born in London, he received little formal education, but read widely and steeped himself in the lore of ancient Greece and the works of Shakespeare, Spenser, and Milton. A victim of tuberculosis, he went to Italy for health purposes, only to die in Rome at the age of twenty-five.

LA BELLE DAME SANS MERCI (page 64)

Three centuries after the ballad of Thomas the Rhymer, Keats rewrote the story as a modern ballad. (See the notes on the ballad, "True Thomas," page 61.) Keats' poem is also about a mortal who is seduced by an immortal, but in his ballad the poet becomes a knight and the Queen of Elfland a "faery's child." The theme of the doom of love is the same as it is in "True Thomas."

La Belle Dame Sans Merci — The Beautiful Lady Without Mercy. STANZA ONE: **knight-at-arms** — member of a military order bound to high ideals of conduct and service. **sedge** — grasslike plant growing in marshes or by the water-side. STANZA THREE: **I see a lily on thy brow** — You look deathly pale. STANZA FOUR: **the meads** — the meadow. **a faery's child** — an enchantress. STANZA FIVE: **zone** — belt or girdle. STANZA SEVEN: **manna** — sweet juice from the manna ash and other plants; also associated with divine nourishment. STANZA EIGHT: **grot** — picturesque cave. STANZA TEN: **thrall** — bondage, enslavement.

ODE TO AUTUMN (page 152)

STANZA ONE: **conspiring** — plotting; the word is interesting since it implies treachery. **their clammy cells** — The honeycombs of the bees are filled to overflowing. STANZA TWO: **thee** — autumn personified. **store** — bountiful supply of produce. **winnowing** — fanning the grain free of chaff. **the fume of poppies** — an opium-like effect. **hook** — reaping tool. **swath** — ridge of grain. **gleaner** — one who gathers the corn. STANZA THREE: **barrèd clouds** — horizontally-striped clouds. **river-sallows** — willow trees by the river. **bourn** — small stream. **croft** — small enclosed area of land. **gathering swallows** — ready for autumn flight.

ON FIRST LOOKING INTO CHAPMAN'S HOMER (page 178)

STANZA ONE: **realms of gold** — classical literature. **western islands** — Ulysses sailed around these islands in the Aegean and Mediterranean. **Which bards in fealty to Apollo hold** — which poets celebrate in praise of the god of poetry. **one wide expanse** — the subjects about which Homer wrote in "The Iliad" and "The Odyssey." **deep-brow'd** — a reference to the beetling brows of Homer which sculptors generally show. **demesne** — kingdom or domain. **Chapman** — George Chapman, an Elizabethan poet and dramatist, translated Homer so clearly and so beautifully that Keats was profoundly moved when he first read it. STANZA TWO: **his ken** — his range of vision. **Cortez** — Actually it was Balboa who discovered the Pacific in 1513, and not Cortez. **Darien** — Isthmus of Panama.

KLEIN, ABRAHAM MOSES (1909 —)

Born in Montreal, he was educated at the universities of McGill and Montreal. Mr. Klein is a lawyer and practises in Montreal. He has served as a lecturer in poetry at McGill. Klein's first poetry was predominantly concerned with Jewish culture, but was broadened with the writing of *The Rocking Chair*, which contains a French-Canadian theme, for which he was awarded the 1948 Governor-General's Award for Poetry. His poetry is rich in diction and imagery, intellectual vigour and emotional warmth.

THE PROVINCES (page 4)

This poem was written before Newfoundland became the tenth province of Canada.

STANZA ONE: **the two older ones** — Ontario and Quebec. STANZA TWO: **the three flat-faced blond-haired husky ones** — the prairie provinces. **the little girl** — Prince Edward Island. **her brothers** — New Brunswick and Nova Scotia. STANZA THREE: **the hunchback with the poet's face** — British Columbia. STANZA FOUR: **the adopted boy of the golden complex** — Newfoundland, which was asking financial aid as a condition of joining Canada, when this poem was first published in 1948. **the proud collateral albino** — the North West Territories. **a game's stances** — set up as in the game of nine-pins. STANZA FIVE: **the forty-ninth** — the line of latitude separating Canada and the United States. **the house with towers** — the Parliament buildings in Ottawa with the Peace Tower. **carillon** — set of bells sounded either from a keyboard or mechanically.

FILLING STATION (page 15)

STANZA ONE: **thorax** — a zoölogical word referring to part of the trunk between neck and abdomen or tail. **rampant** — a word used chiefly in heraldry to refer to the threatening posture of an animal, usually a lion, on its hind-legs with its forepaws in the air. **ambuscade** — lie in ambush. STANZA TWO: **extant** — still existing; the word is usually used in reference to documents. **three-legged horse** — Perhaps the horse is standing on three feet while the fourth is being shod.

LAMPMAN, ARCHIBALD (1861-1899)

Born in Morpeth, Kent County, Ontario, Lampman was educated at Trinity College School, Port Hope, Ontario, and Trinity College, University of Toronto. He entered the Civil Service at Ottawa, and during the 1890's became one of Canada's leading poets.

LATE NOVEMBER (page 41)

The setting of this poem is the Ottawa countryside as it appeared in 1888 when the sonnet was written.

A JANUARY MORNING (page 44)

city towers — buildings of Ottawa. **those northern hills** — the Gatineau hills north of the Ottawa river. **fleeces dull as horn** — clouds dull as the greyish colour of horn.

LARKIN, PHILIP (1922—)

Born in Coventry, England, he was educated at St. John's College, Oxford. He has held posts in libraries since 1943, including university libraries at Leicester and Belfast, and lately has been librarian at Hull University.

LINES ON A YOUNG LADY'S PHOTOGRAPH ALBUM (page 79)

STANZA ONE: **matt** — a dull finish on photographs. **confectionary** —sweetness. **images** — pictures. STANZA TWO: **furred** — in an academic hood or gown trimmed with fur. **trellis** — lattice screen or archway. **trilby** — soft felt: STANZA FOUR: **Hall's Distemper Boards** — bill boards. STANZA FIVE: **your candour** — the frankness or honesty of photography, which is being personified. STANZA SIX: **empirically** — as a result of observation and experiment. **lacerate** — afflict or distress the heart or the feelings. STANZA SEVEN: **at exclusion** — at being left out of your past life.

LAWRENCE, DAVID HERBERT (1885-1930)

Born in Nottinghamshire, the son of a coal-miner, he was educated at Nottinghamshire High School and University College,

Nottinghamshire. On graduating, he taught school, but after completing his first novel, he gave up teaching to follow a literary career. Lawrence travelled abroad most of his life, in such places as Mexico and Italy. He was constantly criticized by the literary representatives of the staid English middle class. He died in Venice from tuberculosis, a disease which he had contracted early in life.

SNAKE (page 96)

The setting of the poem is in Taormina, Sicily, where the poet was living in 1922. STANZA TWO: **carob** — a kind of evergreen found in the Mediterranean area. STANZA FOUR: **Etna** — active volcano on the east coast of Sicily near Taormina. STANZA ELEVEN: **albatross** — This is an allusion to Coleridge's poem, "The Ancient Mariner." In the poem the mariner kills the albatross and later suffers for his wanton cruelty.

HUMMING-BIRD (page 159)

STANZA ONE: **primeval-dumb** — as silent as the first prehistoric period of the world. STANZA TWO: **this little bit** — what was to become the humming-bird. STANZA THREE: **slow vegetable veins** — the stems of the plants, rather than the flowers where humming-birds usually obtain nectar. STANZA FOUR: **the wrong end of the long telescope** — From this end things seem smaller and less important than they really are.

LAYTON, IRVING (1912 —)

Born in Neamtz, Rumania, the son of Moses and Klara Lazarovitch, he came with his family to Canada in 1913, where he attended Baron Byng high school in Montreal and Macdonald College, graduating with a Bachelor of Science in Agriculture in 1939. He received an M.A. from McGill in 1946, whereupon he first became a high school teacher and later a lecturer at Sir George Williams College in Montreal. He received a Canada Foundation Fellowship in 1957. His work, *A Red Carpet for the Sun*, earned him the Governor-General's Award for English Poetry. Mr. Layton lives in Montreal.

ICARUS (page 53)

See the note on Mandel's poem of the same title, page 52, for the story of Icarus and his father Daedalus (page 211).

THE BULL CALF (page 103)

See the comment about the bull as a classical symbol in the notes on William Carlos Williams' poem, "The Bull," page 102.

STANZA ONE: **the promise of sovereignty** — the promise of great power. **the maize** — the corn. **Richard II** — Henry Bolingbroke, later Henry IV of England, deposed Richard II, whose fall Shakespeare interpreted partly as a result of excessive pride. STANZA THREE: **mallet** — hammer. STANZA FOUR: **snuffled on the improvised beach** — The water lapping against the beach made sniffing sounds, like an extemporaneous lament. **sepulchral** — suggestive of the tomb.

LE PAN, DOUGLAS (1914 —)

Born in Toronto, he received his formal education at the University of Toronto and at Oxford. He was with the Canadian Department of External Affairs for several years, and in 1950 was appointed as Special Assistant to Lester B. Pearson, then Secretary of State for External Affairs. In 1948 he published *The Wounded Prince and Other Poems*, for which he received deserved recognition. He taught English at Queen's University, and is now principal of University College, University of Toronto.

A COUNTRY WITHOUT A MYTHOLOGY (page 7)

Mythology — a system of narratives, which were once widely believed to be true, and which serve to explain, in terms of the intentions and actions of supernatural beings, why the world is what it is and why things happen as they do; some critics have affirmed that a mythology is essential as a basis of or background for the development of a distinctive body of literature. STANZA ONE: **taciturn** — not given to much speaking. STANZA THREE: **the abbey clock, the dial in the garden** — the old world of civilized institutions. STANZA SIX: **limpid** — clear, transparent. **Presence** — a spirit or presiding genius of a place; or the ceremonial attendance of a person of high rank. STANZA NINE: **manitou** — Indian word for a god.

CANOE-TRIP (page 18)

STANZA ONE: **fabulous** — given to legend, celebrated in fable. **archipelagoes** — seas with many islands. **slipway** — slope or incline for landing ships or for shipbuilding. **titans** — race of giants said to have ruled the earth before the gods. **Thule** — the name given by Pythias of Massilia to some island north of Great Britain; any faraway, unknown region. **cached** — hidden. **enamelled** — encrusted, adorned. **chimeras** — things of hybrid character, fanciful conceptions. **gules** — red, from the language of heraldry. **circuit** — a trip around, or enclosed area; also a path of current. STANZA TWO: **skirls** — makes sounds that are characteristic of a bagpipe. **cul-de-sac** — blind alley. STANZA THREE: **cumulus** — set of rounded masses of clouds heaped on each other and resting on a horizontal base.

LEWIS, CECIL DAY (1904 —)

Born in Ireland, he was educated at Sherbourne School and Wadham College, Oxford. He edited *Oxford Poetry* with W. H. Auden in 1927, and, after leaving the university, became a school teacher at Oxford, Helensburgh, and Cheltenham, respectively, until 1935. He was employed by the Minister of Information during World War II. After the war, he was occupied with writing, lecturing, and broadcasting. He became Professor of Poetry at Oxford in 1951, and was W. H. Auden's immediate predecessor at that post. He is primarily a poet, but has written novels, detective fiction (under the pseudonym of Nicholas Blake), and stories for children.

DEPARTURE IN THE DARK (page 179)

STANZA ONE: **sweating metal** — suggestive of manacles or fetters. **suicide's grave under the nettles** — the loneliest kind of death. STANZA TWO: **clemmed** — starved, pinched. **as if by an imminent ice-age** — as if the world were going to be destroyed again. **street-**

strolling, field-faring — walks in the city and country. **inveterate hunters** — those things which habitually dull or kill the senses. **mammoths** — large extinct elephants. **presage** — warnings, predictions. STANZA THREE: **passover** — Jewish festival commemorating the liberation of the Israelites from Egyptian bondage, a time when God killed the first-born of all the Egyptians but passed over the houses of the Jews, which were marked with the blood of the sacrificial lamb to distinguish them. After this they were allowed to depart from Egypt. In general terms, the word simply refers to any departure. STANZA FOUR: **Israelites** — an allusion to their departure; see the Book of Exodus. **this land** — Egypt. **a desert of freedom** — the wilderness. STANZA FIVE: **a more tenacious settler** — a more strongly-rooted inhabitant. **in his ripest ease** — when he is exceedingly well-off.

LINDSAY, VACHEL (1879-1931)

Born in Springfield, Illinois, he was educated at Hiram College, the Chicago Art Institute, and the New York Art School. For a short time he imitated the artistic styles of Blake and Beardsley, but soon gave this up to lecture for the Anti-Saloon League, and to preach the "Gospel of Beauty" or art for art's sake in the South. He tramped through the Middle West, exchanging a pamphlet of poems, *Rhymes To Be Traded For Bread*, for his food and a night's lodging. In his poetry he united the chant with what he termed "High Vaudeville", combining religion and ragtime. He introduced into his poetry the blare of the street-corner salvationists, the din of the dance band, and the nervous throbbing of an emerging democracy.

THE KALLYOPE YELL (page 162)

I— **Kallyope** — pronounced kă′/ lĭ / ōp. **Calliope** — pronounced kă / lĭ′/ ō / pī, a steam organ. **sizz, fizz** — the sound of the steam. II — **the Gutter Dream** — the dream of the low-born to become high. **car** — It was transported on wheels. **flags, tent** — the circus. **cockatoot** — cockatoo. **Barnum** — the great American circus owner, partner of Bailey. III — **humanize** — make them care about others. **dour** — severe, stern. **popcorn crowds** — the common people who go to the circuses. **melodiously** — in a way that promotes social harmony. **the sweater's den** — sweat shops; places of employment providing starvation wages and long hours. IV — **every beast** — every enemy and every hardship. V — **a crashing cosmic tune** — a song of universal importance and power. **the spheres** — the revolving, globe-shaped shells in which the heavenly bodies were formerly supposed to be set; their movements were said to produce music or harmony. **softer guise** — less noisy, but still the same song.

LONGFELLOW, HENRY WADSWORTH (1807-1882)

Born at Portland, Maine, he was educated at Bowdoin College at Brunswick, Maine. A short time after graduation, he became a Professor of Modern Languages at Bowdoin. At forty-seven, he resigned his teaching position at Harvard University to devote himself exclusively to poetry. Among his best-known poems are "Evangeline," "Paul Revere's Ride," and "Hiawatha."

THE DAY IS DONE (page 172)

STANZA FOUR: **lay** — short lyric or narrative poem meant to be sung.

LOWELL, AMY (1874-1925)

Born in Brookline, Massachussetts, she came from an illustrious family. James Russell Lowell, the New England poet, was her grandfather's cousin. Her brother, Percival, was the astronomer who mapped the much-disputed canals on Mars. Another brother, Abbott Lawrence, was president of Harvard University. At the start of the first World War she went to London and vied with Ezra Pound for the leadership of the Imagist movement in poetry.

NIGHT CLOUDS (page 176)

porcelain — fragile earthenware with translucent body and transparent glaze. **vermilion** — brilliant red.

MACKENZIE, WILLIAM LYON (1795-1861)

See note under John Colombo, page 188.

MACNEICE, LOUIS (1907-1963)

Born in Belfast of Irish parents, he was educated at Marlborough and Merton College, Oxford. His father was Bishop of Down, Connor, and Dromore. In 1930 MacNeice was appointed a lecturer in classics at Birmingham University. He went to Bedford College, London in 1936, and held the post of lecturer in Greek. He visited America early in 1939 to lecture at various universities, and became Lecturer in Poetry at Cornell University. From 1941 to 1949 he was a member of the BBC, engaged in the writing and producing of radio plays. In 1950 he was Director of the British Institute at Athens, Greece. In 1957 he was given an Honorary D. Litt. from Belfast University.

MORNING SUN (page 171)

STANZA ONE: **shuttles** — cigar-shaped weaving implements that carry weft threads between or across threads of the warp. **posters** — billboard advertisements. **the vocative** — the grammatical case employed in addressing a person. STANZA TWO: **chromium yellows** — bright yellow pigment derived from chromate of lead. **filleted** — striped or banded; in the language of heraidry the word refers to the horizontal division of a shield. **reticulated** — divided into a network of small squares or intersecting lines. **scooped-up and cupped** — as a ball in a tournament. STANZA THREE: **trellises** — lattice screens or archways. **blazons** — gives lustre as heraldric decorations on shields or arms. **scrolls** — ornamental designs; ribbons bearing heraldric mottoes. **bars** — musical phrases; in the language of heraldry, two horizontal parallel lines across a shield. **touché** — a cry in fencing or jousting. **a moving cage** — a float on wheels in a medieval pageant. **a turning page of shine** — like a page in an illuminated medieval Book of Hours. STANZA FOUR: **the red** — the burning part of the cigarette.

MACPHERSON, JAY (1931 —)

Born in England, she came to Canada at nine years of age. In 1951 she received a B.A. from Carlton College in Ottawa. Later she did graduate work at University of Toronto. Her reputation was established with the publication of a collection of poems entitled *The Boatman* in 1957, for which she received the Governor-

211

General's Award. A member of the faculty of Victoria College, University of Toronto, she has also written an account of classical myths for older children, entitled *Four Ages of Man*.

ABOMINABLE SNOWMAN (page 52)

abominable snowman — a hairy creature with supposed human qualities, which was reputed to have lived high in the Himalaya Mountains.

MAGEE, JOHN GILLESPIE (1922-1940)

Born of Anglo-American parents in Shanghai where his father was serving as a missionary, he was educated in Nanking and at Rugby in England. He served with the RCAF in World War II and was killed during manoeuvres on December 31, 1940.

HIGH FLIGHT (page 51)

the footless halls of air — corridors of the sky that have never been traversed by foot.

MANDEL, ELI (1922 —)

Born in Saskatchewan, he joined the Army Medical Corps in 1943. He returned to Canada to complete a doctorate at University of Toronto and later joined the English Department at University of Alberta. His "Minotaur Poems" appeared in a book entitled *Trio*, which was followed by his first independent publication, *Fuseli Poems*, in 1961, and by his most recent collection, *Black and Secret Man*. His poetry applies mythological and anthropological data to contemporary themes.

ESTEVAN, SASKATCHEWAN (page 14)

STANZA ONE: **the mark of Cain** — In Genesis 4: 3-16, God put a mark on Cain for slaying his brother, Abel, saying: "When thou tillest the ground, it shall not henceforth yield unto thee her strength; a fugitive and a vagabond shalt thou be in the earth." **the oldest brother with the dead king's wife** — In *Hamlet* Claudius murdered his brother, the king, and married Gertrude, the dead king's wife. **a foul relation** — To Hamlet Claudius and Gertrude were committing incest. **to feign a summer madness, consort with skulls** — Hamlet did this. **the farmer's chorus** — Because they are predicting doom, the farmers are like the chorus in a Greek tragedy. **harbinger** — one who announces another's approach. STANZA TWO: **returns a sacrifice** — The earth expects a sacrifice once again in return for the act of Cain. **a splintered eyeball** — Oedipus Rex sacrificed himself to stop the plagues and drought of the city of Thebes by blinding himself. **groined** — borne. **scarecrow** — said to have originated as an effigy, which was used instead of human sacrifice during fertility rituals, in order to insure the annual growth of crops. **bawdy** — obscene.

ICARUS (page 52)

This poem is one of a number by Mandel, entitled "Minotaur Poems." The minotaur was a great bull-like beast which King Minos of Crete kept in a labyrinth built by Daedalus. In early Greek mythology, Daedalus was an architect, an inventor, and a creative genius who later tried to escape from King Minos with his son Icarus. Their means of escape was a flight through the air on wings of feathers and wax which Daedalus had fabricated. Although Daedalus arrived safely at his destination, his venture was not successful. Icarus did not heed his father, and flew too close to the sun. The heat caused the wax on his wings to melt and the feathers to drop off, so that he plunged into the waters below and drowned.

as he fell into the sun — like Icarus who flew too close to the sun and later died.

McGINLEY, PHYLLIS (1905 —)

Born in Ontario, Oregon, she was raised on a ranch in eastern Colorado. Later the family moved to Ogden, Utah, where she attended high school. She studied at the universities of Utah and California, and taught English in a New Rochelle, N.Y. high school for four and a half years before turning to full-time writing in Manhattan, N.Y. Her marriage to Charles L. Hayden, a telephone company executive, followed the publication of her first book, *On*

The Contrary in 1934. She was awarded the Pulitzer Prize for Poetry in 1961 for her *Times Three: Selected Verse From Three Decades.*

MOURNING'S AT EIGHT-THIRTY (page 110)

Euphoria — state of bliss. STANZA ONE: **shackle** — fetter, chain. **sanguine** — cheerful, optimistic. **grackle** — an ugly, unpleasant-sounding bird. STANZA TWO: **Phoebus** — the sun. STANZA FOUR: **the Tweed** — English river forming part of the Scottish border. **my bonds** — my investment bonds. STANZA SEVEN: **Sikhs** — members of the Hindu community in India.

A THRENODY (page 125)

threnody — a song of lamentation, especially on a person's death. *The New Yorker* — an American magazine. STANZA ONE: **Tyre, Great Carthage** — ancient cities that met destruction despite their great power, wealth, and glory. STANZA TWO: **democratic front to back** — the front seat, formerly occupied by the chauffeur, is now no longer separated from the back by a glass panel. STANZA THREE: **no minion** — no servant. STANZA FOUR: **wicker hampers** — picnic baskets. **Veuve Clicquot** — wine. **baize** — thick woollen cloth. STANZA FIVE: **cryptic** — secret, mystical. **wife-defeating map** — too difficult for the wife to read. **tooling** — driving in a leisurely manner. STANZA SIX: **to touch a decorous forelock** — to touch the forehead as a sign of respect. **the Warlock** — sorcerer, wizard. **chemise** — woman's undershirt. **Newsboy's Grail** — The hope of ever owning a chauffeur-driven Rolls-Royce was like the often futile search by the Knights for the Holy Goblet in the age of chivalry. **David Niven** — movie actor.

MILTON, JOHN (1608-1674)

Born at the Sign of the Spread Eagle in Cheapside, London, Milton produced a set of poems when a young boy. His father consequently decided that at the age of ten he should be "brought up deliberately to be a man of genius." And indeed Milton was a genius. At Cambridge, where he entered at sixteen, he was unpopular. The boys resented his obvious superiority. There he wrote some of his best early poetry, "Song on May Morning" and "On Shakespeare." Although the last-named poem was Milton's first poem in print, as a short eulogy it received the distinction of being prefixed to the Second Folio edition of Shakespeare. It was published when Milton was twenty-three. Milton's greatest works include *Paradise Lost, Paradise Regained* and *Samson Agonistes.*

THE DEATH OF SAMSON (page 67)

This passage is taken from Milton's long poetic drama *Samson Agonistes.* Read Judges 16 in order to appreciate Milton's talent of writing realistically as well as imaginatively.

SECTION ONE: **occasions** — business. **me** — the messenger, who is speaking to Samson's father, Manoa. **city** — Gaza. **minded** — decided. **degree** — rank. **banks** — sloping ground. SECTION TWO: **State livery** — prison garb. **timbrels** — tambourines. **slingers** — soldiers whose weapon was the sling. **cataphracts** — heavily-armed cavalry. **spears** — spearsmen. **thrall** — slave. SECTION THREE: **for intermission sake** — for a rest or a break. **with amaze** — with confusion and amazement. **with these immix'd** — mixed in among them. **vulgar** — crowd of common people. **scaped** — escaped.

ON HIS BLINDNESS (page 151)

OCTAVE: **light** — sight; also life. **spent** — exhausted; also passed. **talent** — his writing ability. Read the Parable of the Ten Talents for an appreciation of this line (Matthew 25: 14–30). **exact day-labour** — demand the same amount of work as when the poet had his sight. **fondly** — foolishly. SESTET: **prevent** — anticipate, forestall. **thousands** — of angels. **post** — hasten.

NASH, OGDEN (1902 —)

Born at Rye, New York, he was educated at St. George's school in Newport, Rhode Island and at Harvard. He worked with Doubleday and Rinehart publishing houses for a number of years. After the publication of several books of poetry, including *Hard Lines* and *Free Wheeling*, he retired from publishing to devote full time to writing. His poetry is considered to be the best light verse written in the United States today.

LOVE UNDER THE REPUBLICANS (OR DEMOCRATS) (page 66)

First two lines — a parody of the romantic, idealized love poem by Christopher Marlowe, entitled "Come Live With Me and Be My Love." **Anno Donomy** — Anno Dominis. **hauteur** — haughtiness of manner; "class." **nouragement** — nourishment. **quaff** — drink quickly. **Little Italy** — an area in New York City inhabited by Italian immigrants.

KINDLY UNHITCH THAT STAR, BUDDY (page 115)

SECTION I: **crabgrass** — tough weed-like grass that ruins the appearance of lawns. **azalea** — flowering plant. **archangel** — angel of the highest rank. **cherubim** — angelic beings of the second order, gifted with knowledge. **seraphim** — angelic beings of the first order, gifted with love. **process-servers** — sheriff's officers who serve writs and summonses. **bailiffim** — bailiffs; officers under the sheriff in charge of writs, processes, and arrests. SECTION II: **Palm Beach** — expensive resort area in Florida. **the Ritz** — an expensive hotel in New York. SECTION IV: **hitching their wagons to a star** — dreaming big dreams which depend for their realization upon powers higher than the dreamer's own.

NOWLAN, ALDEN A. (1933 —)

Born in Windsor, Nova Scotia, he left school when he was still a youngster. In 1952 he settled in Hartland, New Brunswick, where he became news editor of a weekly newspaper, the *Observer*. He published *The Rose and the Puritan* in 1958, followed by several other books of poetry, including *The Things Which Are* in 1962. Some of his poetry can also be found in *Five New Brunswick Poets,* published in 1962. As a poet and short-story writer, he treats rural life in the Maritimes sympathetically but realistically.

WARREN PRYOR (page 13)

STANZA THREE: **their cups ran over** — an allusion to the Twenty-Third Psalm. **its red dirt** — The soil in some parts of New Brunswick appears red.

PAGE, PATRICIA K. (1917 —)

Born in England, she was brought to Canada at the age of two. She was educated at St. Hilda's School in Calgary, Alberta. In the early 1940's she went to Montreal and became associated with the Preview group of poets, including Patrick Anderson and F. R. Scott. In 1950 she married W. Arthur Irwin, who was then the director of the National Film Board, and in 1953 she went to Australia where her husband was Canadian High Commissioner.

THE STENOGRAPHERS (page 116)

STANZA ONE: **bivouac** — temporary encampment. **forced march** — that which requires a special effort. **midsun** — the middle of the day. STANZA TWO: **the first draft and the carbon** — the first typed copy and the final carbon copy. **the long walk home** — the return home by foot after the ride to the end of the ice-man's route. STANZA THREE: **floats** — buoys. **marrows** — gourd-like vegetables. **the scatter-green vine** — the sea. **wasps' nests** — They resemble buoys in shape. STANZA FOUR: **the voice** — the boss dictating. **but runs like a dog** — The mind wanders. STANZA FIVE: **no wind for a flight** — no opportunity for real love. STANZA SIX: **the terrible calm of noon** — when they stop working and start thinking about their own lives. STANZA SEVEN: **mirror-worn faces** — They are the only ones who look at their faces. STANZA EIGHT: **felt** — firm woollen cloth. **calico** — cotton cloth. **the pin men** — straight pins used in dressmaking.

PICKTHALL, MARJORIE (1883-1922)

Born in Sussex, England, she came to Canada at age seven and was educated at Bishop Strachan School, Toronto. After contributing to *Atlantic Monthly, Century*, and *Harper's* magazines, she published a book of poems, entitled *Drift of Pinions*, in 1913. The first edition of the book was sold out within ten days. Besides other volumes of poetry, she also published three novels.

THE POOL (page 49)

STANZA ONE: **weft of weeds** — weeds interwoven. STANZA TWO: **glooms** — shadows.

PLOMER, WILLIAM (1903 —)

Born at Pietersburg, N. Transvaal, South Africa, Mr. Plomer
was educated at Rugby School in England. He has been a farmer
in Stormberg and a trader in Zululand, and has also lived in Greece
and Japan. Between 1940 and 1945 he served at the British Ad-
miralty. A long list of books, including novels, short stories,
biography, and poetry stands to his credit.

THE DEATH OF A ZULU (page 74)

STANZA TWO: **a ghost** — the dead father of the Zulu child; perhaps
the man was killed in a mine accident or in an uprising against the
whites. STANZA FOUR: **a sudden fear** — the sudden recognition of
the extent of the tragedy, and possibly the sensing of troubles in
the future.

CONQUISTADORS (page 175)

Conquistadors — originally used in reference to the Spanish
plunderers of Mexico, Central and South America. STANZA ONE:
the Rand — highlands on either side of the river near Johannesburg, South Africa. **a plundering city** — Johannesburg. STANZA
TWO: **gilt-edged** — edged with gold, as securities. **veld** — open
country in South Africa. STANZA THREE: **anarchs** — leaders in
disunity. STANZA FIVE: **swashbuckler** — bully. STANZA SIX:
recesses — niches or alcoves. **worked-out reef** — bedrock where
no more gold is left to mine.

PRATT, EDWIN JOHN (1883-1964)

Born in Western Bay, Newfoundland, he was educated at St.
John's College and the University of Toronto. He was Professor
of English at Victoria College, University of Toronto, until his
appointment as Professor Emeritus in 1953. He was elected a
Fellow of the Royal Society of Canada in 1930. Among his best
known works are "Verses of the Sea," and "The Roosevelt and the
Antinoe." In 1952 he published *Towards The Last Spike*, and on
his seventy-fifth birthday was awarded one thousand dollars by the
Canada Council.

NEWFOUNDLAND (page 15)

STANZA ONE: **unsinewed** — loose, lacking in muscular strength.
sluices — gates for controlling the level and flow of water. STANZA
TWO: **sea-kelp** — large seaweed. **gulch-line** — high water mark.
spar — mast pole. STANZA FOUR: **boom** — long spar that attaches
to the bottom of a sail. STANZA FIVE: **insentient** — without feeling.
mastiffs — large, strong watchdogs.

THE ICE-FLOES (page 27)

STANZA ONE: **Foretop, Barrel** — the barrel fixed on the foremast
for the look-out. STANZA TWO: **slob** — softer and more penetrable
ice. **growler** — a miniature ice-berg; the name is taken from the
sound of pieces of ice grinding against each other. **"white harps"** —
young seals. STANZA THREE: **bobbing-holes** — blow holes. STANZA
FOUR: **watches** — work groups. STANZA SIX: **mizzen** — the aft
mast. **pans** — floating areas of ice on which the pelts were heaped.
donkey-winch — a windlass operated by a small engine. STANZA
SEVEN: **"sculped"** — skinned. **sirene** — siren. STANZA EIGHT:
pans — ice detached from the main pack. STANZA NINE: **nave** —
body of a church.

THE SHARK (page 47)

STANZA THREE: **tubular, tapered, smoke-blue** — like the barrel of a
gun. **vulture** — a bird of prey which feeds chiefly on dead flesh.

THE PRIZE CAT (page 48)

The Cat — a symbol for Fascist Italy, which under the leadership
of Mussolini in 1935 invaded Ethiopia, formerly called Abyssinia.
Despite immediate protest by the League of Nations and by
England and France in particular, Mussolini completed his con-
quest the following year. STANZA THREE: **prowling optic parallels**
— eyes. STANZA FIVE: **whitethroat** — the bird mentioned in Stanza
Four.

SEA-GULLS (page 94)

STANZA ONE: **frieze** — broad, horizontal band of sculpture on a
building. **indigo** — blue-violet dye.

RANSOM, JOHN CROWE (1888 —)

Born in Pulaski, Tennessee, he was educated at Vanderbilt University and attended Oxford on a Rhodes Scholarship. On the completion of his formal education, he returned to Vanderbilt University and remained on the faculty for more than twenty years.

BLUE GIRLS (page 81)

STANZA ONE: **sward** — lawn. **seminary** — academy, place of education. STANZA TWO: **fillets** — head-bands. STANZA FOUR: **blear eyes fallen from blue** — eyes that were once blue and clear, but are now dim and filmy.

REED, HENRY (1914 —)

Born in Birmingham, England, Reed was educated at King Edward VI School, Birmingham and Birmingham University. Between 1937 and 1941 he did some teaching and became a freelance journalist. In Birmingham, he was one of a group of poets which included W. H. Auden and Louis MacNeice. He served in World War II and afterwards returned to his writing for a living.

THE NAMING OF PARTS (page 72)

STANZA ONE: **naming of parts** — the naming of the parts of a rifle. **japonica** — ornamental plants. STANZA TWO: **swivel** — a fastening which allows the object to turn freely. **slings** — leather straps attached to rifles for shoulder carrying. **piling swivel** — allows for the free movement of rifles piled with butts on the ground and muzzles interlocked. STANZA FOUR: **breech** — the rear end of a rifle barrel. **easing the Spring** — the poet is punning on the word "spring." **cocking-piece** — the part that sets the trigger for firing.

ROBERTS, SIR CHARLES G. D. 1860-1943)

Born at Douglas, York County, New Brunswick, he was educated at Fredericton Collegiate and the University of New Brunswick. Roberts was a cousin of Bliss Carman. Between 1885 and 1888 he was Professor of English and French at King's College in Nova Scotia. He left teaching for journalism in New York, and then turned to writing as a full-time endeavour. He was awarded the medal of the Royal Society of Canada, and was knighted in 1935. Roberts' poetry is particularly distinctive for its vivid description of the rural countryside and natural beauty of Canada.

THE SOLITARY WOODSMAN (page 9)

STANZA ONE: **bodeful** — onimous, portentous. STANZA THREE: — **cornel** — dogwood. STANZA FOUR: **viburnum** — shrub of the honey-suckle family. STANZA FIVE: **rowan** — scarlet berry of the mountain ash. **bracken** — mass of ferns.

ROBINSON, EDWIN ARLINGTON (1869-1935)

Born in Head Tide, Maine, he was educated for two years at Harvard. At twenty-seven he issued a privately printed collection of verse in 1897, entitled *The Children of the Night*. He went to New York, tried to make a living as an inspector in the New York subway, and almost starved. At thirty-nine he was rescued from poverty by President Theodore Roosevelt, who gave him a clerkship in the New York Custom House. For the last ten to fifteen years of his life, Robinson contended with Robert Frost for the distinction of being America's greatest living poet.

RICHARD CORY (page 141)

STANZA THREE: **in fine** — finally, in short.

ROSSETTI, CHRISTINA GEORGINA (1850-1894)

Born in London of a famous literary family, she lived a quiet and secluded life. She was a devoted Anglo-Catholic, who twice refused to marry because of her religious scruples. She is best known for her religious poetry.

A BIRTHDAY (page 58)

STANZA ONE: **in a watered shoot** — in a tree by the side of a river. **halcyon** — calm. (The word originally referred to a bird which was fabled to have charmed the wind and waves into calm at the winter solstice.) STANZA TWO: **dais** — raised platform for a throne. **down** — fluffy substance usually made of feathers. **vair** — a royal fur used in heraldry. **fleur-de-lys** — the iris flower used frequently in heraldry. **the birthday of my life** — Her love is causing her to be born anew.

SANDBURG, CARL (1878 —)

Charles August Sandburg, who was born at Galesburg, Illinois, has been called the laureate of industrial America. At thirteen he went to work delivering milk. Before he was twenty he had earned a living as a porter in a barbershop, and as a scene-shifter, a truck handler, a dishwasher, and a harvest hand. At twenty-one he fought in Puerto Rico during the Spanish-American War. Upon his return to the United States, he entered Lombard College in Galesburg, Illinois. Sandburg was unknown to the literary world until his thirty-ninth year when he published his *Chicago Poems*. In recent years Sandburg has completed a comprehensive work on Abraham Lincoln, which is considered one of the foremost biographies of modern times.

FOG (page 94)

cat feet — Cats, like fog, are associated with softness, quietness, stealth, danger, and destruction.

CHICAGO (page 120)

STANZA ONE: **Hog Butcher** — Chicago is the largest meat-packing centre in the world. **Player with Railroads** — The city is also a huge railroad centre. **the gunman** — a reference to the power of the gangster in the early days of Chicago.

SCOTT, DUNCAN CAMPBELL (1862-1947)

Born in Ottawa, he was educated at Stanstead College, Quebec. He entered the Department of Indian Affairs at an early age, and became head of the Department in 1913, retiring in 1932. A close friend of Archibald Lampman's, he shared the latter's love of the Canadian northland and its people.

THE FORSAKEN (page 24)

I — **Fort** — trading post. **tikanagan** — cradle board for papoose.
II — **spangled** — filled with stars.

SCOTT, FRANCIS REGINALD (1899 —)

Born in Quebec, he was educated at Bishop's College, Lennox-ville and at Oxford. At McGill University he was both Professor of Constitutional Law and Dean of the Law Faculty. In 1951 he published a book of poems, *The Eye of the Needle*. Scott's contribution to Canadian writing is not restricted to poetry. He was a Rhodes Scholar and Guggenheim Fellow, and is a writer of authority on Canada's economic and social problems. He retired as Dean of the McGill Faculty of Law in 1964.

TRANS CANADA (page 50)

STANZA ONE: **pulled from our ruts** — a description of take-off from the air strip. **wider prairie** — the sky. **like a pile of bones** — Regina was founded on the site of a huge pile of buffalo bones. The creek that runs through the city bears the Indian name for a pile of bones, Wascana. STANZA TWO: **Skeena salmon** — British Columbia salmon which go up the Skeena river to spawn; many die in attempting to ascend the rapids of the river. **Six-way choice** — north, east, south, west, up, and down. STANZA THREE: **a still** — The word is used here as it is in reference to a "still-life" painting, or to a "still" photograph. **troughs** — hollows between waves of cloud. STANZA SIX: **an I land** — On earth, man's own worth is all-important, whereas in the sky he is an insignificant speck.

SHAKESPEARE, WILLIAM (1564-1616)

Born at Stratford-on-Avon, he was educated at the Stratford Grammar School. His father was Mayor of Stratford, and his mother was of landed gentry. He went to London and was the principal actor and playwright in the "Lord Chamberlain's Players," later called "The King's Men." It was for this company that he wrote the plays which immortalized him. Shakespeare the poet wrote one hundred and fifty-four sonnets. Sonnets one to one hundred and twenty-six were dedicated to his patron, a mysterious Mr. W. H. The remainder were addressed to the "Dark Lady."

BLOW, BLOW, THOU WINTER WIND (page 105)

This song can be found in Act Two, Scene Seven of *As You Like it*.

STANZA ONE: **keen** — sharp. **rude** — rough and cruel. STANZA TWO: **nigh** — near; hence, deeply. **benefits forgot** — unremembered favours or kind acts. **warp** — throw out of shape.

SHALL I COMPARE THEE (page 150)

lease — rental, as opposed to ownership; thus, impermanence. **gold complexion dimm'd** — sunlight dulled by clouds or rain. **every fair from fair . . .** — Everything beautiful gradually loses its beauty. **by chance** — by accident. **nature's changing course** — the cycle of the seasons, or of birth and death. **untrimm'd** — made less decorative. **that fair thou ow'st** — that beauty you own, rather than merely rent. **this** — this poem.

SHELLEY, PERCY BYSSHE (1792-1822)

Born at Field Place, Sussex, of a family of rural gentry, he was educated at Eton and Oxford, from which he was expelled for the publication of the pamphlet, *The Necessity of Atheism*. After the suicide of his first wife, he left England in 1817, a virtual exile, and took up residence in Italy. He was drowned when his boat was wrecked in the Gulf of Spezia off the western Italian coast.

THE CLOUD (page 91)

STANZA ONE: **their mother's** — the earth's. **flail** — instrument for beating or threshing. STANZA TWO: **lightning my pilot** — the lightning in a storm seems to direct the movements of the cloud. **genii** — ruling or presiding spirits, representing the force of electricity in the clouds and the force of the water. **he** — the lightning by way of the thunder. **Spirit** — one of the genii or forces of electricity. STANZA THREE: **sanguine** — blood-red. **rack** — sailing or floating cloud. STANZA FOUR: **orbèd** — spherical, globular. **woof** — one of the threads used in weaving. STANZA FIVE: **burning**

zone — halo of light. **chair** — chariot. **sphere-fire** — sunlight. STANZA SIX: **my own cenotaph** — my tomb, which is "the blue dome of air."

OZYMANDIAS (page 112)

visage — face, countenance. **these lifeless things** — the broken pieces of the monument. **the hand that mocked them** — the sculptor's hand. **the heart that fed** — Ozymandias' heart.

SMITH, ARTHUR J. M. (1902 —)

Born in Montreal, he was educated at McGill and the University of Edinburgh. In 1943 he received the Governor-General's Medal for poetry. Mr. Smith is a Professor of English at Michigan State University.

THE LONELY LAND (page 3)

STANZA ONE: **spume** — froth, foam. **windrift** — derived from "spindrift", which refers either to spray blown along the surface of the sea or to light, feathery clouds. STANZA THREE: **dissonance** — discordance, harsh tones.

SOUSTER, RAYMOND (1921 —)

Born and educated in Toronto, he worked in a bank for two years. In 1941 he joined the RCAF. He was co-editor of *Contact*, an international magazine of poetry which was discontinued in 1954, and is associated with Contact Press, a non-profit organization for the advancement of modern Canadian poetry.

ROLLER-SKATE MAN (page 114)

STANZA TWO: **Queen Street** — street in downtown Toronto. STANZA THREE: **flotsam** — wreckage found floating. **jetsam** — goods thrown overboard and washed ashore.

DOWNTOWN CORNER NEWS-STAND (page 119)

you — the newsie. **Stars** — copies of *The Toronto Daily Star*. **Telys** — copies of *The Toronto Telegram*. **King and Bay** — street corner in Toronto's business section.

SPENDER, STEPHEN (1909 —)

Born in London, England, the son of a journalist, he was
educated at Oxford. With W. H. Auden, Louis MacNeice, and C.
D. Lewis, he was considered an English poet of the avant-garde
school. As in the case of Auden, he was associated with various
left-wing movements and visited Spain during the 1937 civil war.

THE EXPRESS (page 123)

manifesto — public declaration, usually by a ruler, state, or body
of individuals. **the elate metre** — the high-spirited rhythm. **trajectories** — paths of bullets.

STEVENS, WALLACE (1879-1955)

Born in Reading, Pennsylvania, he was educated at Harvard
University and the New York Law School. He was admitted to the
bar in his twenty-fifth year, and practised law in New York State.
Twelve years later he moved to Connecticut, where he specialized
in insurance law, and in 1934 became vice-president of the Hart-
ford Accident and Indemnity Company. Stevens' poetry has been
compared to the works of abstract painters, and his volume, *The
Man With The Blue Guitar,* was, by implication, a kind of homage
to Pablo Picasso, the controversial and versatile contemporary
painter.

THE MAN WITH THE BLUE GUITAR (page 136)

I — **a shearsman** — one who cuts away and therefore trans-
forms. **a tune beyond us, yet ourselves** — a tune that is intensely
beautiful or moving, yet not removed from reality. II — **I cannot
bring a world quite round** — Reality keeps changing so quickly
that I am unable to capture a moment of it as it is. **a blue guitar** —
one that changes things, rather than showing them exactly as they
are.

TENNYSON, ALFRED, LORD (1809-1892)

Born at Somersby in Lincolnshire, England, Tennyson was a
precocious child. He composed blank verse at the age of eight,
wrote hundreds of lines in imitation of Pope at ten, and at twelve

made an analysis of Milton's *Samson Agonistes*. At Cambridge, he formed a friendship with Arthur Hallam, a brilliant young man with a promising future. Hallam died suddenly when travelling on the Continent. His death greatly affected Tennyson, who considered it a great personal loss, and so he began to question the existence of God and the purpose behind the universe. In 1850 he published one hundred and thirty poems reflecting these feelings, under the heading of *In Memoriam*. In the same year, on the death of Wordsworth, he was appointed Poet Laureate. He is considered the greatest English poet of the second half of the nineteenth century.

THE SPLENDOUR FALLS (page 69)

STANZA ONE: **the splendour** — the splendour of the sunset. **castle walls** — Ross Castle on Lake Killarney in south-western Ireland, where Tennyson heard the echoes of a bugle blowing, during a visit in 1848. STANZA TWO: **scar** — steep face of rock. **purple glens** — the heather on the glens. STANZA THREE: **they** — the echoes. **our echoes** — our enduring qualities, our posthumous influence.

THE LADY OF SHALOTT (page 142)

I — **the wold** — open, uncultivated country. **dusk** — make dim or shadowy. **imbowers** — encloses in an inner room. **margin** — edge. **shallop** — light open boat. II — **village-churls** — peasant boys. **Abbot** — head of an abbey of monks. **pad** — easy-paced horse. III — **brazen greaves** — shin armour made of brass. **red-cross knight** — one who devoted his life to a search for truth. **gemmy** — adorned with precious stones. **blazon'd baldric** — a belt hung from the shoulder to the opposite hip, decorated with heraldic colours. IV — **seer** — prophet. **burgher** — citizen.

THOMAS, DYLAN MARLAIS (1914-1953)

Born in Swansea, Wales, the son of a school teacher, he was educated at the Swansea Grammar School, and later became a newspaper reporter. During World War II he worked with the BBC. He died suddenly while on a lecture tour in the United States.

FERN HILL (page 77)

STANZA ONE: **dingle** — a deep dell, usually shaded with trees. **apple towns** — towns with apple orchards. **windfall** — an apple blown down by the wind, which is unusually bright and rosy. **river of the windfall light** — the flood of sunlight that causes the windfall apples to ripen so beautifully. STANZA TWO: **green** — young, inexperienced, growing. STANZA THREE: **the tunes from the chimneys** — the sound of the wind in the chimneys. **fire** — glowing life. **rode to sleep** — emphasizes the child's vitality even at bedtime. **night-jars** — night birds. **ricks** — haystacks. STANZA FOUR: **like a wanderer** — as if the farm had gone away and come back during his sleep. **Adam and maiden** — as fresh and innocent as the beginning of life. **after the birth of the simple light** — a reference to creation. **spellbound** — as if the horses are also caught in the spell of creation. STANZA FIVE: **sky blue trades** — joyful activities. **out of grace** — out of a state of innocence; also, out of time's favour. STANZA SIX: **up to the swallow thronged loft** — to the memories of youth. **the farm forever fled from the childless land** — the farm which is not at all the same as it was during his childhood. **green and dying** — young, and yet at the same time advancing toward death. **I sang in my chains** — I was nevertheless joyful in my bondage to time.

WHITMAN, WALT (1819-1892)

Born at West Hills on Long Island, New York, he had very little formal education, and at twelve became an apprentice in a print shop in Brooklyn. He entered the writing and editing field of journalism, and became a strong voice in the political and social problems of the day. His leading book, *Leaves of Grass*, was worked upon for fifteen years before he published it in 1855. It received little notice, except by Ralph Waldo Emerson. Whitman's great faith in himself and his work is shown by the fact that he nevertheless revised and expanded the book nine times during his lifetime. Because of his intense faith in democracy and the dignity of man, he is ranked among the great American poets.

SONG OF MYSELF (page 83)

I: **I celebrate myself** — as a representative of all mankind. **assume** — take upon oneself. **in abeyance** — held back, waiting. **hazard** — chance. II: **distillation** — process in which vapour of perfume is changed into drops. **filter** — purify to obtain the essence. III: **the flag of my disposition** — a freely waving symbol that represents his feelings and attitudes. **the handkerchief of the Lord** — that which draws attention to God. **a uniform hieroglyphic** — secret symbol with the same meaning wherever it is found. **Kanuck** — Canadian. **Tuckahoe** — Virginian. **Cuff** — Negro. **the beautiful uncut hair of graves** — associated with death. IV: **journey-work** — work done by a qualified artisan. **pismire** — ant. **chef d'oeuvre** — masterpiece. **to stagger sextillions of infidels** — to overwhelm billions of unbelievers. **gneiss** — laminated rock of quartz, feldspar, and mica. **esculent** — fit for eating. **stucco'd** — plastered or cemented. **plutonic** — igneous; that is, derived from the action of internal heat. Pluto was the Greek god of the underworld. **mastodon** — large extinct mammal like an elephant. **auk** — northern sea-bird with short wings used as paddles. V: **sidle** — slow, sly walk. VI: **my gab** — my chatter. **scud** — vapoury driving clouds. **effuse** — pour forth.

WILBUR, RICHARD (1921 —)

Born in New York City, he was educated at Amherst and Harvard Universities. In 1957 he became Professor of English at Wesleyan University.

THE DEATH OF A TOAD (page 75)

STANZA ONE: **verge** — extreme edge, border. **sanctuaried** — hidden in a private spot. **cineraria** — bright-flowered plant. **ashen** — greyish. STANZA TWO: **rare original heartsblood** — The toad is associated with original forms of animal life, being an amphibian. **wizenings** — creases or wrinkles. **banked** — confined, so that they appear to be unmoving. STANZA THREE: **ebullient** — boiling, exuberant. **toward lost Amphibia's emperies** — back to the time when amphibians ruled the world. **castrate** — deprived of vigour after having been cut. **steer** — direct its course.

WILLIAMS, WILLIAM CARLOS (1883-1963)

Born in Rutherford, New Jersey, he received his formal education in New York, Switzerland, and the University of Pennsylvania, where at twenty-four he graduated in medicine. At twenty-six he published his first volume of poetry, and thereafter pursued the dual career of poet and doctor.

THE BULL (page 102)

STANZA ONE: **a drag** — heavy iron peg or shoe used to prevent the escape of animals or vehicles. **the bull is godlike** — a classical representation of the gods; e.g., King Minos of Crete kept a minotaur or bull-like creature which had the power of a god, while Zeus, the king of the gods, disguised himself as a bull to seduce Europa. STANZA FOUR: **Olympian** — a reference to Mount Olympus, the home of the gods. STANZA FIVE: **lacquer** — varnish; hence, the glossiness of the bull's coat. **glossy pinetrees** — They have taken on a special glow from the bull's presence. STANZA SIX: **ivory or glass** — suggestive of purity, beauty, and rarity. **milkless** —emphasizes the creature's maleness. STANZA SEVEN: **hyacinthine** — The hyacinth is a classical symbol of immortality.

WORDSWORTH, WILLIAM (1770-1850)

Born in Cumberland, he was educated at Hawkeshead Grammar School and at Cambridge University. He travelled extensively in France, and became an advocate of the principles of the French Revolution. He devoted the greater part of his life to poetry, particularly about nature, and introduced the use of common speech as poetic language. On Southey's death in 1843, he was appointed Poet Laureate.

UPON WESTMINSTER BRIDGE (page 82)

Westminster Bridge — From the bridge could be seen the landmarks of London, including the Thames River, St. Paul's Cathedral, Westminster Hall, and the Houses of Parliament.

THE SOLITARY REAPER (page 133)

STANZA TWO: **the farthest Hebrides** — islands in northern Scotland. STANZA THREE: **Will no one tell me what she sings?** She is singing in Gaelic, a language that he cannot understand. **numbers** —music, from the mathematical element in rhythm.

THE WORLD IS TOO MUCH WITH US (page 150)

a sordid boon — a poor favour. **have glimpses** — obtain some insight; also, see visions. **Proteus** — a Greek sea god who tended the seals and rose at noon to bask on the rocks. **Triton** — son of Poseidon, the sea god, who blew on a sea shell to raise or calm the sea. **Wreathèd** — twisted.

YEATS, WILLIAM BUTLER (1865-1939)

Born at Sandymount, he was educated in Hammersmith and Dublin, Ireland. He studied at the Royal Dublin Society to be a painter, but soon gave this up for writing. Yeats was a senator in the Irish Free State. His devotion to Ireland was so intense that he at times lived in the wildest counties to integrate himself with the problems of his land. With the collaboration of a few others, Yeats was responsible for the renaissance of culture in Ireland; he helped to establish and develop not only the Gaelic League, but also the Irish Literary Theatre or Abbey Theatre. In addition, he wrote dramas and lyrics involving Irish legendry, perfecting folk-lore as well as developing a powerfully symbolic poetic style equal only to that of T. S. Eliot in this century.

THE MAGI (page 129)

The Magi — an ancient priestly caste of Persia; the Three Wise Men who journeyed to Bethlehem; all those who are waiting for a Second Coming. **the pale unsatisfied ones** — dissatisfied with the present Christian era. **hoping to find once more** — waiting for a Second Coming. **uncontrollable mystery** — the turbulence that ushered in the Christian era. **the bestial floor** — the stable at Bethlehem.

THE LAKE ISLE OF INNISFREE (page 161)

Yeats was in the city of London, observing an advertisement for soda pop, when he was reminded of the beauty and quietude of Innisfree.

STANZA ONE: **I will arise and go now** — from the Biblical story of the Prodigal Son. **Innisfree** — Lough Gill in County Sligo, Western Ireland. **wattles** — interlaced rods and twigs plastered with clay. **nine** — mystical number of perfection. STANZA TWO: **to where the cricket sings** — to evening. **a purple glow** — the reflection of the heather in the water. STANZA THREE: **it** — the lapping of the water.

INDEX OF AUTHORS

234

ROSS SHEPPARD
ENGLISH DEPARTMENT

17 18   126960   84 83